THE SEARCH FOR PEACE

Extemporaneous talks given by Osho in Mumbai, India

THE SEARCH FOR
PEACE

OSHO

Early talks by Osho, first published 1998 in Hindi as *Trisha Gai
Ek Bund Se*. These talks are given by Osho to live audiences. The
complete OSHO text archive can be found via the online OSHO
Library at www.osho.com/Library

OSHO MEDIA INTERNATIONAL
New York—Zurich—Mumbai
an imprint of
OSHO INTERNATIONAL
www.osho.com/oshointernational

Library of Congress Catalog-In-Publication Data is available

Printed in India by Manipal Technologies Limited, Karnataka

ISBN: 978-0-99123-781-4
This title is also available as an eBook ISBN: 978-0-88050-613-7

Contents

Preface

A man of peace is not a pacifist; a man of peace is simply a pool of silence. He pulsates a new kind of energy into the world, he sings a new song. He lives in a totally new way – his very way of life is that of grace, that of prayer, that of compassion. Whomsoever he touches, he creates more love energy.

The man of peace is creative. He is not against war because to be against anything is to be at war. He is not against war, he simply understands why war exists. And out of that understanding he becomes peaceful. Only when there are many people who are pools of peace, silence, understanding, will war disappear.

But withdrawal is not the way to attain peace. Withdrawal is escapist. Withdrawal can give you a kind of death, but not peace. Peace is very alive. Peace is more alive than war – because war is in the service of death, peace is in the service of life. Peace is very alive, vibrant, young, dancing.

Osho
Zen: The Path of Paradox, Vol. 2

Chapter 1

Who Am I?

My beloved ones.

What is humanity? What is a man? – a thirst, a call, a yearning.

Life itself is a call; life is a yearning; life is an aspiration.

But aspirations can be for hell as well as for heaven; the call can be for darkness as well as for light; the yearning can be for the false as well as for the truth.

Whether we know it or not, if we have asked for darkness, we will continue to be troubled. If we have chosen the false, we will go on being disturbed. If we have chosen wrongly, it is impossible to be at peace. Peace comes like a shadow, born from a longing for that which is right. Peace is born out of right longing.

A seed wishes to flower. If it flowers, it is filled with bliss, but if it cannot, it will experience anguish and pain. The river wishes to become the ocean. If it can reach the sea, if it can merge with the infinite, it will find rest. If not, if it meanders into the desert, it will be in turmoil, troubled, in pain.

A sage has chanted: "O God, lead me from darkness to light; from unconsciousness to consciousness; from the false to the truth." That indeed has been the hope, the call, of all humanity. If on the journey of life we find ourselves becoming more peaceful, know that we are moving toward the hidden core of life. But if we are becoming more disturbed, then we are moving in the wrong direction, the opposite direction.

Turmoil and peace are not an end in themselves. They are only signs, indicators. A calm mind indicates that the direction we are moving in is the direction toward life. A troubled mind indicates that the path we are moving on is not the path to take, that the direction we are moving in does not lead to our destination – where we are heading is not where we are born to go.

Turmoil and peace are signs of whether our life has developed in the right direction or the wrong direction. Peace is not the goal. Those who make peace their goal can never attain peace. Turmoil can also not be eliminated directly. The man who attempts to stop the agitation becomes even more agitated. Turmoil is an indicator that life is moving in a direction it was not meant to go; peace tells us that we are on a path toward the temple that is the ultimate aim of life.

A man has a high temperature, a fever; his body is burning. The heat of the body is not the sickness; the body's heat only indicates that there is sickness inside. When the temperature is normal, it is an indication that there is no sickness inside. The raised temperature itself is not the disease; it is an indicator of a disease. However, having a normal body temperature is also not health; it is only a sign that the internal life is in a healthy state. If a man forcibly tries to bring down the temperature of his feverish body, he won't be free of his disease – he may even die.

No, fever of the body does not have to be removed. The fever is a friend, informing us about the sickness within, giving news of the disease. If the body doesn't run a temperature but remains diseased within, a man won't even know that he has fallen sick, that death may come.

Agitation is the fever – the sickness, the heat – that engulfs the consciousness and informs you that you are taking your life where it should not be going. Feeling calm is a sign that the fever has gone, that life is now moving in the direction it was meant to go. It is essential to understand this fundamental truth. Then, during the coming four days, our journey in search of peace will be totally clear.

Do not long for peace and do not try to remove agitation. Understand the agitation, and transform your life. Transformation of life automatically opens the door to peace. It's just like when a man goes for a stroll in a garden. As he approaches the garden he becomes aware of the cool breeze surrounding him, the scent of the flowers enveloping him, the song of the birds in his ears. He is certain then that he is near the garden – the songs of the birds, the cool breeze, and the scent of the flowers are all there.

Peace is a sign that you are close to the ultimate reality; it is the scent of the flowers growing in its garden. Agitation is a sign that we have turned our backs on the ultimate reality. Hence, fundamentally, what a man sees as the reasons for his turmoil are not really the reasons at all. If a man thinks that he is disturbed because he does not have wealth, then he is mistaken. Wealth may come, but the disturbance will remain. A man may think he is disturbed because he does not have a large house. He may get the house, but the disturbance will remain; in fact it will even increase a little. When there was no house, no wealth, at least there was the consolation "I am disturbed because I do not have a house, do not have money." You get the house, you get the money, and yet the disturbance remains. Then your life will become even more agitated.

This is the reason why a poor man's agitation is never as great as a rich man's. The poor man is never able to understand a rich man's misery. Without becoming rich, it is difficult to understand that a rich man does not even have the poor man's consolation "Because I am poor, I am not at peace" – at least there is an identifiable reason why he is not at peace. "One day my poverty will end and I will be at peace."

But up to now, no man has attained peace by getting rid of his poverty. Poverty goes, peace does not come, the agitation just increases because for the first time you come to know that obtaining wealth has no relationship at all to removing agitation. Then even the hope that if you become wealthy you will be at peace disappears.

That is why the more a society prospers the greater is its discontent. Today, perhaps no society is as discontented as the American society. In the history of mankind, no society, no country has ever possessed the kind of wealth America possesses. It is very strange that although they have all this, they are still discontented. If in this country we are not at peace, it can be understood, for we have nothing. But having or not having anything has no relation at all to being at peace or in turmoil.

Man's existence is made up of a body, a mind, a soul. The body has needs. If these are not fulfilled, life becomes painful. The body has needs – food, clothes, shelter – and if these are not met, the journey of life becomes painful. All the time the body will tell you: "I am hungry, I am naked, I don't have medicine, I am thirsty; there is no water and there is no food." All the time the body will complain about this, and the feeling of something lacking fills life with pain. Remember: life is filled not with agitation, but with pain.

It is possible that a man may be in pain but not be agitated, and it is also possible that a man may not have any pain but still be agitated. In fact, this is often what happens. The man in pain is not even aware of any discontent. He is so involved in his pain that he has neither the luxury nor the opportunity to think of any discontent. When the pain disappears, for the first time the awareness comes that there is discontent within. The poor man is in pain. The rich man is discontented.

The body is filled with pain, but once the needs of the body are met, the pain disappears. But even so there is no experience of joy on the level of the body. It is important to understand this: the body can contain pain, but joy can never be in the body. Certainly, if pain disappears, if there is no pain, we mistake it for joy.

If a thorn pierces your foot, there is pain, but if there is no thorn, there will be no joy. You will not go around announcing to the neighborhood that today there is no thorn in your foot, so you are happy; that today you do not have a headache, so you are happy. If we have a headache, we will be in pain, but if there is no headache, we will not be happy. It is very useful to understand that at the level of the body there is never anything like joy; there is only pain or the absence of pain. People mistake the absence of pain for joy. The body can feel pain or the absence of pain, but it can never give joy. That is why those who live at the level of the body never know anything of joy. They know only pain and relief from pain. If they are hungry, they feel pain; once the hunger is satisfied, the pain disappears. These are the limitations of the body.

Beyond the body, within the body, is the mind. The condition of the mind is exactly the opposite. The mind also has its needs, the mind has its demands, and the mind has its own hunger and thirst. Literature, art, philosophy, music – all are desires of the mind, the hunger and thirst of the mind. They are food for the mind. But someone who has not read the poetry of Kalidas will not be in pain. Or someone who has not heard the sitar from a great maestro will not feel pain because of it. If it were so, man would surely die from pain, because there are so many things in the world of the mind of which we know nothing.

In the world of the mind, what you do not know, what you have not experienced, does not cause pain, but knowing it creates joy. If you have an opportunity to hear a sitar performance, it brings joy. If you had not heard it, there would have been no pain. If you do not read poetry, haven't heard it recited, haven't understood it, there is no pain. But if you hear it, it brings joy.

Joy is at the level of the mind. If joy has been experienced but later it is not attained, a lack of joy is felt: people mistake that for the pain of the mind. At the level of the body, there is no joy, only the absence of pain. And at the level of the mind, there is only joy or a lack of joy, nothing like pain.

But the mind has one more quality: the joy that exists at the level of the mind is fleeting, never more than that. The pleasure that the mind finds once, it does not find in its repetition. If today you heard someone playing the veena and then he plays for you again tomorrow, you will not experience the same joy tomorrow as you experienced today. The day after, the joy will be even less. If you have to listen to it continuously for another ten days or so, what was experienced as joy on the first day will now begin to feel like pain. And if you are forced to listen to it for three to four months, you will feel like banging your head against a wall, feel like running away – you will not want to hear it any longer.

At the level of the mind, new pleasures are continuously sought after. The body always seeks old pleasures, never new ones. If the body is made to experience new things every day, there will be problems. If the body is used to sleeping at ten o'clock every night, then it will always want to sleep only at ten. And if food is taken at eleven o'clock every morning, then the body will only want to eat at eleven. The body is like a machine, it wants the same thing every day. It wants repetition, wants no change in its routine. Any man who has to subject his body to changes every day will find his body in great pain.

Modern society has harmed the body grievously. Modern society wants the body to behave like new every day, but the poor body wants to keep to the old. That is why people living in villages appear to be far healthier than a man living in a city. His body has to adapt daily to new demands, new needs, and new rules. This becomes a problem for the body because it does not have the understanding to be able to renew itself every day. It keeps demanding the old.

The mind wants something new every day; it is not satisfied with the old. As soon as something becomes even a little old, the mind revolts and has had enough. It wants a new house every day, a new car every day – and if it could have its way, it would want a new wife every day, a new husband every day. That is why in societies which have developed by gradually giving priority to the mind, the divorce rate goes on increasing. No society built on the basis of the mind can be stable. The older countries in the East live with the body as the basis; the modern countries of the West have started living with the mind as the basis. The mind wants something new every day.

I have heard that in America there is an actress who has married thirty-two times. It is beyond our imagination. Wives in our country pray to the gods that even in the next birth they should get the same husband. If a wife in America were to pray – although this will never happen – the prayer would be: "Please make sure that I do not get that man again." One cannot be sure of a next birth and that is why – the wife is smart – she wants to change him during this lifetime.

The actress that I spoke about, the one who married thirty-two times, when she married for the thirty-first time, she realized after about fifteen days that she had already been married to that man. The changes had been so fast and frequent that it took fifteen days before she recognized whom she had married. Wives in our country, even after five or ten lifetimes, will catch hold of their husband and ask: "Don't you remember?" They will remember for many lifetimes.

The mind desires something new, every day. That is why the mind becomes bored with the old and is troubled. If you meet a loved one and embrace him, in the beginning you will feel very happy. But if that friend is very affectionate and does not end the embrace, then after a few minutes there will be great uneasiness. That initial burst of joy disappears. And if that man is totally mad – as lovers often are – and keeps you locked in an embrace for half an hour, you will feel like strangling yourself or him. But what has happened? When this man came and embraced you, it gave great joy, so what is the problem now? Why this uneasiness? The mind becomes bored. The body is never bored; the mind always becomes bored.

You will be surprised to know that a thing like boredom affects no animal in the world except man. You will never see buffalos becoming bored. Nor will you have seen a crow or a dog sad, bored, fed up. No, except for man, no being becomes bored. Boredom is not possible for other beings, for they all live at the level of the body. At the level of the body there can be no boredom; it happens only in the mind. And the more a mind develops the greater is the boredom. That is why the countries of the East are not as bored as the countries of the West. As boredom increases, in order to break the monotony, it becomes necessary to look for new sensations every day.

You will also be surprised to know that man is the only being who becomes bored and man is the only being who laughs. Except for man, no animal in the world laughs. If you are walking along the road and a donkey begins laughing, you will be so flabbergasted that you will not be able to sleep, because we do not expect an animal to laugh. One who does not become bored also does not laugh. Laughter is a way of eliminating boredom. That is why when you are bored, you hope to meet a friend, have a few laughs, so that the boredom can be reduced.

Man needs so many ways to entertain himself because he becomes so bored during the day that he needs continuous entertainment. Then even the entertainment becomes boring and new ways to be entertained are needed. When boredom spreads from all sides, war is needed. With war, monotony is destroyed.

You might have seen how people's faces lit up when India and China – or India and Pakistan – went to war. Their eyes were so bright. They all appeared to be so fresh and alive. Why? Life is so full of boredom that any activity, any disturbance, is welcome. If there are riots somewhere, even then life becomes a little more active, a little brighter, the slumber breaks a little; it seems as if something is about to happen, there's something new to see. Otherwise everything has been seen, everything has happened already and is being repeated, the mind becomes bored, and the mind becomes restless.

This happens only to you. No animal becomes bored, no animal laughs, and keep in mind that no animal except for man commits suicide. Man can even get so bored with life that he puts an end to it. Even the process of ending life can provide novelty. Even the ending of life can be a new stimulant, a new sensation.

There was a case lodged against a man in Sweden. He had stabbed a stranger sitting on the beach. In court he was asked: "Did you have any quarrel with this man?"

He replied: "There is no question of any quarrel. I had never seen this man before. I hadn't even seen his face. I stabbed him from behind, in the back."

The judge said: "You are very strange. Why did you stab him?"

He replied: "I was so bored that I wanted something

to happen in life. I had never killed anyone before, so I wanted to see what that felt like. I don't want to say anything more in my defense. If I am to be hanged, that would make me happy because for me there is nothing left worth seeing in life. I have seen everything. Death alone is new."

In the West, murders are increasing, suicides are increasing, crimes are increasing. The reason for this is not that the West is becoming more criminal. The sole reason for this is that in the West, life has become so full of indifference and boredom that resorting to crime seems to be the only way to get rid of them.

I have just heard of a new game that has developed in America. It is a very dangerous game – and when societies are bored they develop these kinds of games. The game is that two cars, with their wheels centered on the dividing line on the road, race toward each other at full speed and power. With the cars racing toward each other at full speed, the first one who moves his car out of the way for fear of an accident loses; the one who does not wins.

Now if two cars are headed directly toward each other at a speed of one hundred miles per hour, there is great danger to life. Who will move out of the way first? Whoever moves loses. This society has arrived at the limit of boredom. Now there does not seem to be any excitement unless life itself is put at stake.

That is why when a society begins to get bored, liquor is discovered, gambling is born – and the stakes are high. Whenever in any society there is a lot of gambling, understand that the boredom is great. Now without high stakes, without facing any danger, there seems to be no possibility of anything new happening.

In the world of the mind, things become old every day; the mind cannot experience joy for more than a moment. A moment passes and the joy turns to pain. At the level of the body, there is pain, but no joy, only the absence of pain. At the level of the mind, there is joy but only momentarily; in a moment it fades and is gone. That's why, even though we may madly desire something and are willing to put everything at stake for it, if we get it, we suddenly become sad.

You wish to buy a very beautiful house. Buy it, and you will find that suddenly everything is over. That enthusiasm, that running around, that excitement, that happiness which existed in the search for the house, all vanish as soon as you buy the house. You will be disappointed as soon as you get what you wanted because it brings only momentary happiness. After a moment everything will feel old again, things will be as they were.

There is joy at the level of the mind, but momentarily. And the man who lives only between the body and mind will be forever agitated. How can a man who has not had a glimpse of permanent bliss be at peace? And at both the level of the body and the mind it is not possible to have a glimpse of permanent bliss.

But, in a sense, people living on the plane of the body will still appear peaceful – peacefully dead. Peace is of two kinds: one alive, living; the other deathly, dead. Go to the graveyard. There, too, there is peace, but that is the peace of the grave. There is peace because there is no one there who can be at unrest.

Buddha was camping outside a village called Amravan with his monks. He had come with ten thousand monks. The king of the village was told by his friends of Buddha's arrival. They urged him to meet Buddha, so the king went to meet him.

It was evening and beginning to get dark. They had nearly reached the place where Buddha was staying with his monks, when suddenly the king drew his sword and said to his friends: "It seems you want to trick me. We are so near the place where ten thousand people are supposed to be staying, and yet there is no noise. It appears so peaceful. Are you leading me into a trap?"

His friends replied: "You are not familiar with Buddha and his followers. You have so far seen only the peace of the graveyard; now see the peace of the living. There are ten thousand people in those gardens. Please come, do not mistrust us."

With each step he took in the dark the king was becoming more fearful – *was* he being led into a trap? But his friends kept saying: "Please come, please don't worry; there really are ten thousand people there. Ten thousand people, but a silence as if no one were there."

When he reached, he bowed his head to Buddha's feet and exclaimed: "I am astonished, ten thousand people! There are ten thousand people sitting under the trees and there is absolute silence as if there is no one around."

Buddha then replied: "It seems you have only known the peace of the graveyard. There is also the peace of the living."

In one sense, people who live at the level of the body are at peace. Animals are at peace, they do not feel unrest. Some men, too, will be at peace merely by living at the body level. They will eat, put on clothes, sleep, and again eat, put on clothes, and sleep. But this kind of satisfaction is not peace; it is merely absence of awareness. You are not aware. It's as if inside you are dead; your state is like that of a dead man.

Someone once said to Socrates: "You are so much at unrest, Socrates, that it would have been far better if you had been a pig. What is the use of being Socrates? Pigs walk around the edge of the village and are so much at peace. They lie in gutters, eat whatever they can: how happy and peaceful they appear."

Socrates replied: "I would prefer to be a dissatisfied Socrates than a satisfied pig. No doubt a pig *is* satisfied, but it is because it does not thirst for anything beyond the body; it hears no other call in life. It's almost as if it does not exist. I am certainly dissatisfied because I hear a call drawing me toward the peace I am seeking. Until I find it, I will be at unrest. But I choose this unrest. And I consider it to be my good fortune."

The state of those among us who are satisfied at the level of the body is not very different from that of the animals. An animal means: satisfied at the level of the body, at rest; a man means: unrest at the level of the mind; a divine being means: peaceful at the level of the soul.

Between the body and the soul is the mind. In the world of the mind, bliss is glimpsed only momentarily. Even though it's only for a moment, where does this glimpse come from? This momentary glimpse comes from the soul. If the mind is silent, even for a moment, then in that moment bliss descends from the soul. In that silence, peace is glimpsed. Just as when lightning flashes on a dark night, everything is lit up for a moment and then again plunged into absolute darkness. The mind is darkness, but if for a moment it is silent, in that moment the light of the soul hidden behind it is revealed.

You meet someone you love. For a moment your

heart stops, for a moment your thoughts stop, and you draw him into an embrace. For a moment everything stops. A glimpse of the soul enters you – but only for a moment. Then the mind starts working again, the mind starts racing again, filled with thoughts. The world comes alive again and you find yourself again standing just where you were. The man you have embraced now seems boring; you feel like withdrawing. The peace and the joy that you experienced when you embraced the loved one were not because of the beloved. He was only the medium; it had come from within you.

When music silences the mind temporarily, you sense peace within. If you think that this peace is on account of the sitar that you are listening to, you are mistaken. The sitar only provided the opportunity, and the mind was free and became silent. As soon as the mind is silenced, the peace that is within is sensed. Peace always comes from within, bliss always comes from within. But if the mind finds an opportunity outside, momentarily it is possible for it to be in silence. It is in this state of silence that something flows within. The mind is silent and something flows inside. That is why when the mind is silent for a moment – the flow is only for a moment – all disappears.

But there is a soul beyond the mind. And it is the direction of this soul, the path that leads to this soul, the consciousness that is required to enter the soul, which is the very same consciousness that leads to bliss, peace, and divinity.

How can we flow in this direction? I will try and explain with a story.

I was born in a very small village. There is a small

river that flows near the village. Most of the year it is just an ordinary river, but during monsoon it becomes very powerful. During the rains, being a mountain river, a lot of water flows through it and it is almost a mile wide. Then the river flows in full fury and it is very difficult to cross. But I have loved that river from my very childhood and it fascinated me to cross the river during the rains.

I must have been fifteen or sixteen years old and on numerous occasions had crossed that river during the rains with my friends. But a thought came to me that I should cross the river alone, in the darkness of the night. It was very dangerous because the current was very strong. I decided to cross it at two o'clock in the night, in pitch darkness. The more dangerous something is, the greater is its attraction. It was a very dark night. I went down into the river. I struggled to reach the other bank, swam for almost two miles, struggled, and tried everything, but it seemed almost as if the other bank was not there. In the darkness, the other bank was not even visible.

I was exhausted. It seemed as if that night I would not survive. I made one more attempt, one last attempt. The waves were rough, the night dark, and the other bank not visible. Now even the bank I had started from was too far away. There was no sense in turning back; it was quite possible that the far side might now be closer than the bank I had started from. The strong current of the river was taking me along – I had already covered two or three miles.

I made one final attempt. The more I tried, the more difficult it was to reach the far bank. Then, for a moment, it seemed as if death had come. My limbs refused to function, my eyes closed. I thought death had arrived, that everything was finally over. After about two hours, when my eyes opened, I found myself lying on the other bank. But something had happened during these two hours – I want to talk about that.

It was as if I was reborn; as if I had died and returned. As soon as I felt I was dying – death had come – I decided that since death was now inevitable, let me calmly look at it and know it. I closed my eyes and let my limbs go limp. It was, of course, very dark outside, but it seemed as if even within I had entered some pitch dark cave. I had never before seen such absolute darkness...

It's dark outside, but the darkness is not absolute. On the outside, there is light too, but that too is not absolute light. The darkness outside is muted; the light outside is also muted. For the first time I experienced the darkness about which the sages must have prayed: "O God, please lead us from darkness to light." Up to then I had thought that the sages must have been talking about the normal darkness outside when they asked to be led from darkness to light. And I used to think that this darkness could so easily be removed by switching on a light. What was the need to trouble God about such a simple matter?

Many times I was surprised at the foolishness of the sages. When a simple lamp could be lit to dispel the darkness, what was the need to pray to God about it? They must have been unscientific, probably did not have much intelligence, otherwise they could have simply lit a lamp and solved the problem. There was no need to pray to anyone to remove the darkness.

But on that day, I realized for the first time that there is a darkness that cannot be removed by the light of a lamp, a darkness where no lamp can go. For the first time I understood the nature of the darkness for which the prayer was meant. I had not known that darkness until then. Artists do not have a color so dark. It was difficult to even imagine that there could be such absolute darkness.

There is always some light outside. If the moon is not there, there are stars. If the sun is setting and clouds cover the sky, even then some sunrays will pass through the clouds. The truth is that darkness outside is only relative, partial, never total, never absolute. For the first time the realization dawned on me of what absolute, total darkness is, of what total night is. I felt panic rising in that darkness; then I understood why man is so afraid of the dark outside.

There *is* no danger in the darkness outside, so why does a dark night give rise to such fear? And why, for thousands of years, has man been worshipping fire? Then I felt that perhaps the darkness outside gives rise to some faint recollection of the darkness within. Otherwise there is no reason to be afraid of the darkness outside. Perhaps the lighting of a lamp or a fire, or the worshipping of fire, are really part of the attempt to remove the darkness within.

For the first time I saw the darkness. I was walking into that darkness at full speed – it kept getting darker and darker – and my whole being was agitated. It must have all happened in a moment. It could not have taken longer, but for time there are varying scales, varying perceptions, varying measures.

When you are awake, you measure time by the movement of the hands on the clock. But this is not an exact measure. If you are happy, the hands appear to move very fast, but if you are in pain, then they seem to move very slowly. If someone in your house is dying and you are at his bedside, see how slowly time passes.

It seems as if the clock has stopped, as if the hands have stopped moving, are stuck in one place. The night seems to keep getting longer, it feels as if it will never end. The clock is moving at its own pace. It is not concerned if someone is dying in your house, but it appears as if it has totally slowed down.

If you meet a loved one whom you have not seen for a long time, the clock begins to race. It does not seem to move second by second but seems to be jumping hours. The night passes so quickly. It was evening just a while ago, and now it's already morning. So fast? How did this happen? It feels as if the clock has become an obstacle to your love. The whole world has put obstacles in the way of your love, and now the clock has become one, too. The night has passed so swiftly.

On the outside, the pace of time changes with happiness and pain. The greater the pain, the more slowly the hands of the clock seem to move. The greater the happiness, the faster the hands of the clock will move. In absolute sorrow, the hands of the clock will freeze, time will stop. In total happiness, the hands of the clock will revolve so fast that you will not even see the movement. Again they will appear to be frozen.

And, inside and outside time differ. During the day, you doze off for a moment and dream that you are marrying, then you have children, your daughter has grown up and you are looking for a groom for her; you find a boy, your daughter is getting married... Then suddenly you wake up, look at your watch and see that you have dozed off for barely a minute. You had napped for just a minute. Then how did so much happen within a minute? You got married, had children, your daughter grew up, you found a boy for your daughter, and were getting her married with all the song and dance? Then suddenly you woke up. Only one minute had passed on the outside, so how did such a long and eventful journey happen inside?

In a dream, the measurement of time is different, the speed of time is different, and when you are awake it is again different. This I realized on that day. I was going within so fast, everything was happening so quickly, as if it was beyond time. My entire being was struggling in terror – how to escape from this darkness? How can I escape, how can I get out of this darkness? And that day for the first time, my mind was filled with thirst, with the prayer, "O God, lead me from darkness to light."

Until you experience this darkness, you will not know this thirst. In the coming few days, we will try to experience a little of this darkness within. One who is not even aware of the darkness inside will not cry for any light, will not weep, will not plead for any light inside.

...I do not know for how long I remained in that darkness. Then, in frustration, I started banging my head against a wall. Today, narrating this, it seems it was for a very long time. I was banging my head very hard and screaming "Open the door, open the door!" There was no one saying it, there were no words inside, but my entire being was screaming.

There *is* nobody inside actually shouting to have the door opened; there are no such words within. But the entire being, every pore, is screaming "Let me out, open the door." I have heard that Jesus said "Knock, and the door shall be opened." I used to think "Can it be as simple as this? Knock and the doors will open?" And these are the doors to the ultimate reality. Just knock to open the doors? If it was so simple, any passerby would knock. But that day I understood what was meant by knocking.

I was screaming with every breath, every pore of my body, with my whole being – not in words but emotions. If the soul itself knocks on a door, the door will surely open. Then the doors opened into a slightly bigger cavity. Until now it had been like a tunnel, a cave, very narrow cave from where I was frantic to escape, but now the cave was a little bigger with a faint light. The mind relaxed a little.

But when I opened my eyes and carefully looked into the faint light I could see a great amount of activity and commotion. Many shapes of different colors could be seen, running around furiously. And as I moved forward there was a large market, very crowded, with people of all kinds, and a variety of objects. But the objects on display were unique; I had not seen such things before...

I have heard that the Greek philosopher Plato used to say objects are on the outside, but their beauty and form are within. I have heard that the world of the mind contains within it forms of all objects that exist. Outside I can see you. If I shut my eyes, I am still able to see you. With eyes shut, you are locked outside. Then who is it that I am able to see inside? Obviously, some form of yours – some thought form, some shape imprinted on the mind – has remained inside.

There are many thoughts imprinted on the mind, racing here and there from all sides. It is like a carnival, a jamboree. At the first stage there is pitch darkness, no turmoil, but at the second stage there is a faint light and tremendous turbulence and noise. The voices are eardrum-splitting loud. It is necessary to escape from such shrill sounds or else a man can go mad. Later the thought came that perhaps the first stage of darkness was at the level of the body and the second at the level of the mind.

At the level of the body, there is pitch darkness and at the level of the mind, there is great commotion. The body is a tunnel, a tiny cave; the mind a huge expanse. But this expanse is very crowded, with lots of colors, lots of sounds, lots of smells. Everything you have ever known or experienced is all there, it never dies. All that you might have lived or experienced, even in infinite lifetimes, is all there. The mind is an amazing museum of all your life-times. All the people who were your friends, all those who were your enemies, whatever you've heard, whatever you've said, whatever you've experienced – everything that has ever happened to you – is all collected there. In this huge expanse, there is this large crowd, and a cacophony of sounds and voices. This can be frightening and drive you mad.

Is this the illusion that is surrounding you from all sides and fragmenting you? And is this the voice urging you to keep moving, keep moving, the race is on? Then the closed door is in front of you. You start banging your head on it, screaming, until finally the door opens.

There is also a third world where there are no limits, no darkness, no light, no sound. A world where there is no darkness and no light because the light that we know is just a form of darkness, and the darkness that we know is just a form of light. There is something there that the mind hesitates to label *light*, for this light is nothing in comparison to what we know as light.

...But for a moment a wave of bliss spread through

my being, and then I returned, my eyes opened, and I found myself lying on the bank. For a moment it seemed as if I had been dreaming. I could not believe what had happened. I thought about it a lot, but there was nothing concrete; it must have been a dream. But the dream kept chasing me. With a lot of effort I kept exploring the dream. Then, gradually, what had happened that day during that confrontation with death started happening naturally.

In the coming three days, I want to take you on that journey also.

The first voyage – on the plane of the body. The second voyage – on the plane of the mind. And the third voyage, the third journey, is on the level of the soul.

If even once you have a faint glimpse of that ray, it cannot be forgotten. It becomes the nucleus around which transformation of life begins taking place. Once a ray of this light is encountered, life is transformed; it's like being reborn. One ray fills life with a sense of peace. Then irrespective of the problems encountered in life – whether somebody stabs you in the chest, or cuts off your head, or burns you with fire, insults or praises you, abuses you or puts a garland around your neck – none of them matter. It's as if everything is happening in a dream. At the core, where there is absolute calm, none of this makes any impact. There, the calm, the bliss – whatever is there – remains unfragmented and whole, unmoved, unshaken. The experience of reaching this point and its spreading through your being is what peace is.

Peace is not an event of the mind. All the psychiatrists of the West have made a fundamental error in this respect. Western psychiatrists have tried to bring peace to man via his mind. They will never succeed. Peace is not something of the mind. At the level of the mind, at best there can be an adjustment, a compromise, but never peace.

Peace is of the spirit, a reflection of spiritual attainment.

That is why in the West they know nothing of peace. Instead, innumerable efforts are being made to understand the mind, its sicknesses, its thoughts, its tendencies, to understand the full state of the mind and to try and organize it more effectively. But all these efforts are not going to lead toward peace. Peace is something that is achieved when the mind is transcended, when you can go beyond the mind, when the mind has become a thing of the past.

At the level of the mind, there is nothing like peace No matter how much the mind is organized, the most that can happen is that it may be better able to tolerate turmoil – it can never be at peace. Being able to endure agitation is one thing, being at peace is a totally different thing. Being healthy is one thing, being able to tolerate sickness is quite another.

Today, whatever progress is being made in psychology, whatever is being done in psychiatry, the best it can do is to make people better able to face the tumult within; it can never give them inner peace. Man becomes peaceful only at the third level – the level of the soul.

Why does man become at peace only at the level of the soul? As I said, the body is hungry, it needs food; the mind is hungry, it needs joy. In the same way, the soul is hungry, it needs the ultimate reality: the food of the soul. And the day you step into this third level, you realize what the ultimate reality is. As soon as you meet with the ultimate reality, you experience the bliss of peace pervading your entire life. Once you experience this, you cannot ever lose it again. The truth is: it is not lost even now, we are just not aware of its presence. It is not possible to ever lose it; within us it is always present.

It's as if a treasure is hidden inside somebody's house, but he keeps walking round and round on the outside, wandering on the outside. The more he wanders, the more he forgets the way inside and the wandering becomes a habit, a pattern. Now only this path is seen and he keeps moving along this beaten track. Gradually his recollection fades so much that he does not even remember that there was any treasure inside. And because he is wandering outside, he keeps asking everyone he meets: "Where is the treasure? What am I looking for? What do I hope to find? I know nothing." Yet all the time he is circling the treasure.

Man's condition is similar to this, which is why he is in turmoil. He is not able to obtain what belongs to him because he doesn't know that he already has it. He has no awareness of what he possesses. His whole life is wasted in wandering aimlessly.

Unrest means: wandering outside; peace means: entering within.

But how does one go inside? Going inside is actually very simple. *Simple* does not mean easy. It does not mean it can be attained cheaply. The truth is that there is nothing more difficult than to be straightforward and simple. There is nothing more complicated, more arduous, than being simple. It's easy to be complicated, and very difficult to be simple because in simplicity the ego gets no satisfaction, but in being complicated the ego gets a huge boost. The ego dies in simplicity because it gets no nourishment.

I have heard that Meister Eckhart said somewhere: "To be ordinary is the most arduous thing." It's very difficult to be ordinary. When Eckhart died, someone said he was a most extraordinary man, an exceptional man. When asked why, he replied: "Because he was such an ordinary man." He was extraordinary because he was so ordinary. It's very difficult to be ordinary. It seems strange that we think of a man being exceptional only because he is so unexceptional.

Similarly it will seem strange to hear that being simple is difficult. Do not mistake simple for easy. And yet it *is* easy, for simplicity is your nature, and it cannot be difficult to get what is your nature. It cannot be difficult to get what is already within us; it cannot be difficult to know who we are. But it has become very difficult because for many lifetimes we have been walking a path that has no relation to where we want to go. And through walking on this track for so many lifetimes, the habit has become so deeply ingrained that we are unable to turn our heads toward ourselves; it's as if our necks are paralyzed.

If we ask a man whose neck is paralyzed to turn his head and look back, he will say "It is very difficult," and we will counter "What is the difficulty? Just turn your head and see." He will reply "What you say is correct, but my neck is very stiff, and cannot turn. Unless I turn around totally, my neck will not turn; the neck alone cannot turn." But man wishes to look back by just turning his neck, which is why he is unable to go back. The whole man, the total man, has to turn back. Only then can he return.

That is why Tao, the universal law, is the complete transformation of life. It is not just turning the neck.

The poets say: "Just bow down and you will see." No picture within can be seen just by bowing down your neck a little. It's not just the neck that has to bow down, but the whole man. It's a complete turning, a complete conversion. For this, not just the neck has to bend, not just the limbs, but the whole man has to bend. And how the whole man can bend is what I will talk about now.

But before that… We will be sitting here in meditation every day – also today we will be sitting in meditation for fifteen minutes at the end – so I will explain a little about the meditation. And then I will try to explain how, from tomorrow, we can begin this journey – step-by-step. But understanding is not as important as it is to experiment. We will experiment with this now and I'll explain how.

We will now begin an experiment in meditation. It's a very simple experiment; it is an attempt to awaken the part within you that is sleeping. Normally, if someone is sleeping, we wake him up by calling him. If we know his name, we can call out his name. But what will we do if we do not know his name?

We know nothing about the one who is sleeping within. We certainly do not know his name. Then there is only one thing to be done – to ask with all our totality "Who am I?" And if we ask "Who am I?" with all our being, then slowly, gradually, the sleeping parts within us will begin to awaken. The day this question reaches the core of our being, up to the third door, then the answer to the question "Who am I?" begins to come from whosoever is within.

Those who have said "*Aham brahmasmi* – I am the ultimate truth" have not sat in some library and reproduced it from a book. They have asked themselves "Who am I?" And they have kept on asking, they have immersed their lives in this question, in this quest for who they are. Like an arrow, this question kept penetrating deeper and deeper, until from within they found the answer.

But all of us are very smart. We ask why we should work so hard. In the books it is written that we are truth. We will just remember that. Why should we struggle? We will just memorize it. If the question arises, we will just say "I am truth. I am the soul." These are false answers – false not because those who said this were liars, but false because they are not *your* answers. Whatever is not your answer is false. We have learned from books what we are, but know nothing at all about it.

No, to reach to the ultimate reality we will have to ask, we will have to seek – and the day we find our answer, it will be *the* answer. As soon as we get our answer, everything changes. It's one thing when a blind man gets his eyesight back, and something totally different when a blind man hears from others about light and begins repeating that there is light. It has no relevance at all to his regaining his sight.

So here we will ask "Who am I?" And it cannot be a dead questioning, lifeless, mechanical. It cannot happen this way because the question has to pierce many deep layers within.

If you are lost in a jungle on a dark night, all by yourself, will you ask normally, calmly, if there is anyone under the trees: "Is anyone there?" No, you will not ask the question like that, your question will come from your whole being: "Is anyone there? I have lost my way!" Every flower in the jungle, every hillock, every ridge will echo with your question. You will put all of yourself into that question.

Losing our way is much more than losing the way in the jungle. After all, how long can you remain lost in the jungle? By morning you will return home. Even without asking, you will find your way back. The sun has to rise. But the jungle we are lost in spans many lifetimes. We have no knowledge of how many lives we have been lost for. But we ask so lifelessly if there is a way out that it seems as if we are not really interested.

This asking has to be total. It cannot be partial, fragmented, in small bits and pieces; it can be only total. And this is a guarantee: any man who asks with all his might can get the answer this very day. What is the need to wait until tomorrow? But we have never really asked; we have never looked. We have always hoped that from somewhere we will be able to borrow the answer.

No! In the search for truth, nothing can be borrowed. In the search for bliss, there is nothing that we can get from another – it has to be our labor, our resolve, our power. And this is also the measure of how authentic our demand is, of whether we really deserve what we are asking for. There is only one measure of value in this search: whether we have put all of ourselves into it. This meditation has only one condition. It has to be done not gradually, not slowly, not as a routine, but absolutely totally, as if life itself depends on it. It is possible that we may not be alive the next moment; it is possible that after a moment the breath may not return. Even if this happens, we should not say that we came back without knowing ourselves. This is where we are at present.

Mahavira said once that you can never know when a morning dewdrop on a blade of grass will roll off with the breeze. Human life is like that: a dewdrop on a blade of grass, a slight breeze and it rolls off. Man's life is surrounded by so much insecurity, so much instability, so much danger – there is no guarantee that the next moment will come. But when man goes in search of himself, he goes as if there is no hurry, as if he has all the time in the world. It cannot continue like this.

When we meditate here during the three days, I hope you will immerse yourself in it totally, with full commitment of your breath, of your heartbeat, of your body, of your mind. The more totally you immerse yourself, the deeper inside you will be able to go. The more completely you jump in, the deeper you will go. What else needs to be done? Nothing much, it's a very small thing.

When we sit down, all of us should sit down comfortably with the fingers of the two hands interlocked tightly, so that the body's full force is put into the question. The pressure on the hands will indicate the intensity with which the question is being asked. The hands may become stiff, stonelike. With all ten fingers interlocked in your lap, sit down comfortably. Then we will shut our eyes. After shutting the eyes, our total attention should be focused on the spot exactly between the two eyes. Why on the center? In the coming days, I will try and explain the reason for this and what the result of this is. Both eyes will be shut, but in such a way that even with closed eyes we will be looking inside ourselves from the spot between our eyes. The hands will remain locked, the spine straight, the body loose.

First sit down like this. Hands locked, spine straight. The spine should be straight because the straighter it is, the more forcefully the question will arise. You may have noticed that whenever you are filled with enthusiasm or vigor the spine automatically straightens up. You will have noticed that during a fight a man's spine is never bent; it automatically straightens. When it's a matter of your entire life, the spine will automatically straighten.

So, spine straight and hands locked. Those hands will be the measure of the fervor with which you are asking the question. The greater the intensity, the stiffer the hands will become; it will become difficult to open them. They will be totally clenched as if they have no strength to open again. And both eyes will remain shut with the attention focused on the central point between them, the point where, between the two eyes, the nose begins. The eyes will be directed at the point where the bridge of the nose starts.

Then move inside yourself: lips closed and with the tongue touching the palate. When the lips are closed, the tongue will automatically turn to the palate, closing the mouth totally. We are not to speak with our mouths; we now have to speak with our life energy from inside. The question to be asked is "Who am I?" The question has to be asked so quickly that between two questions there is no space left: "Who am I, who am I, who am I, who am I?" Like this: so forcefully and so intensely that there is no strength at all left in the body.

It is possible that the body may begin to tremble. It is possible that tears may flow from the eyes, that you might want to cry. When the body puts all its strength into something, all this is possible. You need not prevent anything. Let whatever is happening, happen. Just ensure that you go on asking the question – keep asking as if your whole life is at stake. "I will ask and I will know that which is within me."

We will do this experiment for fifteen minutes. After the experiment, our session today will come to an end.

So now let us all sit down. Those who are standing,

please sit down where you are. Nothing will happen if you sit down. Even if your clothes get a little soiled, it is not a problem. You should sit down because if anyone is standing, it will be an obstruction for the others – hence please sit silently wherever you are. No one should talk. And make sure not to disturb anyone else.

Right, now straighten your spine. Lock your hands. Shut your eyes. Focus all your attention between your eyes, the eyes are closed. Now bring your attention to the spot between the eyes as if with our eyes closed we are looking at the spot between the eyes. Right, lips closed. Now, with full intensity begin asking "Who am I? Who am I?" Rapidly, quickly, swiftly and with full intensity. Keep asking, with all your strength "Who am I? Who am I?" Not softly, but with all your power because the question will go deeper inside, depending upon the intensity with which you ask.

Who am I? Who am I? Who am I? Who am I? Ask rapidly, with all your power, all your strength. The question comes from every beat of your heart, from every breath of your body. The hands remain clenched, the spine remains straight. The body might tremble, tears may flow, but put all your strength... As the force increases, you will find yourself becoming calmer. A deep sense of calm will spread inside.

Who am I? Who am I? Who am I? No, not gradually but with full intensity. Who am I? Who am I?

Do not come to me later and say nothing happened. With full power...

Who am I? Who am I? Who am I? Who am I? Who am I? Keep on asking; go deeper and deeper, like a penetrating arrow, deeper and deeper.

Who am I? Who am I? Who am I? Let the whole

body tremble… Who am I? Use all your strength… Who am I? Who am I? Who am I? Who am I? Who am I? Who am I? Who am I? Who am I? Who am I?

You will begin to feel a deep sense of peace. Who am I? Who am I? Who am I? Who am I? Who am I? Who am I? Who am I? Who am I? With full strength, with all the power you have; let there be a storm. The whole creation should ask: Who am I?

So many souls collectively asking and without any result? Who am I? Who am I? Who am I? With full fervor… Let whatever happens, happen.

Who am I? Do not bother about anyone else, only yourself. Who am I? Who am I? Who am I? Who am I? With every breath, every heartbeat. Nothing should be remembered except this one question: Who am I?

Who am I? Who am I? And deeper and deeper; a profound sense of peace will spread. The more forcefully you ask, the greater will be the sense of peace. The more intensely you ask, the greater will be the sense of calm.

Who am I? Let the question shake your entire being, your whole life is shaken: Who am I? Like when a tree is shaken so hard, even its roots are shaken. Who am I? Who am I? Who am I? I have to find out, I have to know, I have to reach… Who am I? Who am I? Who am I?

Ask, ask, ask… Only one question should remain; only this question should remain: Who am I? Who am I? Who am I? Who am I? Who am I? Lost in the darkness, asking: Who am I? I have lost my way, don't even know my self. Who am I? Have to know, have to find out… Who am I? Who am I? Who am I? Who am I? Who am I?

Five more minutes, with full intensity: Who am I?

Who am I? Put all your strength into it. Who am I? With all your force... Who am I? Let there be nothing in reserve; it should not feel as if you are making a half-hearted attempt. Who am I? Who am I? Who am I? Who am I? Who am I? Who am I? One thump on the door... Who am I? Who am I? Like banging on a closed door... Who am I? Who am I? Who am I? Pitch darkness... Who am I? Who am I?

The faster you ask, the calmer the mind will get. Who am I? Just one echo... Who am I? Who am I? The last two minutes, with all your strength, with full power: Who am I? Who am I? Who am I?

The final minute: Who am I? Who am I? Who am I? Who am I?

The mind will become calmer and a deep sense of peace will spread inside, like when everything becomes quiet after a storm. Who am I? Who am I? Who am I? Who am I?

For the final time: Who am I? Who am I? Who am I? Leave it only after reaching the peak. Who am I? Who am I? Who am I? Who am I? Who am I? Who am I?

Leave it... totally drop it. Be calm... Drop it. Slowly, slowly open your eyes. Sit silently for a few moments... slowly open your eyes, then slowly open your hands. Slowly open your eyes...

I have to tell you about three small points; once I have told you, we can stand up.

The first point is that when I come and go, no one should touch my feet. I am nobody's guru, and I do not believe that anyone is anyone else's guru or disciple. Hence, no one should touch my feet. I am also not a saint or a mahatma. The attempt to be a saint or a mahatma seems extremely childish to me. Therefore, there is absolutely no need to treat me with reverence, admiration or veneration. You show more than enough respect toward me when you listen attentively to what I say. You do not even have to accept it. Just think about it and experiment. If it is right, it will stay; if it is not, it will drop.

The second thing I want to say is: if someone comes to me, it's in my nature to give love. Those who are afraid of love should not come near me. My condition is a little like that of Plato...

Plato had become old, and throughout his life he believed that love was prayer. In his old age he contracted leprosy. Even then when people came close to him, he would embrace them. The people were very afraid. Who wants to be embraced by someone with leprosy? Therefore they stopped coming to him. Plato used to ask: "Why don't people come to meet me now?"

Out of hesitation people would keep quiet. Then some friends finally gathered courage and said: "Your body is affected by leprosy but you hold people's hands, embrace them, and sometimes even kiss them on the forehead. People are scared to come to you."

Plato replied: "Ah yes, I keep forgetting that I am a body too. I don't even remember that my body now has leprosy."

Similarly, try and avoid coming near me because I also do not know that I am a body. I also forget that my body is that of a male. It's not too much of a problem when men come near me, but when women come near it becomes a problem. Therefore please take care and do not come close to me. It is difficult for me to change my nature now, but you can be more understanding and stand a little away from me.

When I came here, I was told that a member of parliament from Baroda had made some statements about me. On hearing them, I realized that what he had said was correct...

A lady had come from Delhi. She was a professor at some university and in no way less intelligent than the member of parliament. She came up to me and very persuasively said that it would be her great fortune if she could stay with me.

"I have been waiting for years in the hope that sometime I might be able to spend at least two days with you."

I replied: "You are mad; you could have come anytime."

She stayed with me. I was not aware that her remaining would become such a big issue. If somebody had come to me and said that her staying with me would cause them great trouble, I would not even have bothered with them. Or I might have said: "You also come, come and stay with me, sleep here." But nobody came.

I left to go to a meeting. The next day these people threw out all this lady's luggage. When I returned, I saw her standing there, crying. She said: "I have been grossly insulted, and many uncivilized things have been said to me."

I replied: "This is very strange."

My friends then informed me: "When this lady came she embraced you. It is highly uncivilized and shows poor character that a lady should embrace you."

I told them that it would have been far better if they

had told me this, but to throw out her belongings and say things to her was also very wrong, very uncivil. And when I came back here, I learned that they had given an interview to the newspapers about this incident.

That is why the thought came to me that I should inform you of this. I do not keep a record of who comes to meet me – man or woman, I am not bothered. In the future, it will also be very difficult for me to keep track of this. Therefore it is better to stay a little away from me.

It is not good to create problems for members of parliament, as these poor officials are trying to maintain the character of the country. It is because of them that the character of the country is so first-rate; otherwise it would have been destroyed. Our country can boast of such high moral character and behavior only because of them. And people like me will always spoil character, therefore it is better to stay away from such people!

So my second request is that it will be very good if you greet me only from a distance. Even for a personal meeting with me, please think very carefully. In the first instance, there should be no need for such meetings because whatever I have to say I say it here, so there is nothing to ask me separately. But I realize that there may be some issues which need to be discussed individually. But these MP's do not want anyone to speak to me separately. If it was limited only to men, then maybe it would be acceptable, but if any women want to come and meet me, then it becomes a huge problem. So women should definitely not come to ask me anything separately. Now this is not my fault. They need to understand that their being a woman is to blame; their being born in India is to blame.

Whoever wants to meet me alone should think

carefully, and be aware that a meeting is being sought with a person who hasn't a good character. So please think very, very carefully before coming to meet me as it creates a lot of problems, difficulties, and trouble for people.

A problem is always a reflection of our mindset; the difficulties are from our mindset. People whose consciousness is filled to an extreme with lust will see nothing but lust in this world. It is not possible for them to see anything else. Dr. Ram Manohar Lohia has written a book in which he has asked a question...

When Buddha went to the city of Vaishali, the city prostitute called Amrapali, known as the bride of Vaishali, fell at Buddha's feet and asked for initiation. Dr. Ram Manohar Lohia has raised the question: when Buddha saw such a beautiful woman, what kind of thoughts would have passed through his mind? What kind of a fluttering would he have felt?

It is very amusing. Dr. Lohia wants to know what kind of a fluttering and what kind of thoughts would have passed through Buddha's mind. But Dr. Lohia was also an MP, and of course officials such as he should worry. After all, the country's character depends upon them.

When Vivekananda came to India, Sister Nivedita's accompanying him to Bengal became a problem. A sannyasin, and with a woman! They were not even aware that for a sannyasin there is no more man or woman. But it became a big problem, a very troublesome, difficult issue.

Magdalene, a woman, came to Jesus, fell at his feet and washed his feet with her tears. From that very day all the trouble started. For Jesus it became a big problem. Why had he allowed a prostitute to touch his feet? Now, for Jesus, can anyone be a prostitute? And for Jesus, is there any difference between man and woman? But of course Jesus is in the wrong. Our parliamentarians know and understand better what is right and wrong. And the parliamentarians of that day crucified Jesus. Socrates was accused of being characterless and corrupting the youth.

Vivekananda was a young and handsome man when he went to Ramakrishna Paramhansa. The rumor started that Ramakrishna loved handsome boys. It was fortunate for Ramakrishna that there were no parliamentarians in Dakshineshwar, otherwise he would have known what real trouble is!

So it is fitting. The MP's have not made any mistake, they have done the right thing, said the right thing, and it is not their fault either; they must say these things. I had told them that we should talk separately. But they said no, it would not be right to speak about this issue separately. Perhaps now they themselves will feel that this should have been discussed privately. I will definitely go to Baroda during election time and urge people to vote for them, otherwise the moral character of the country will be destroyed. Keep voting for them; otherwise there will be no hope for the country's moral progress!

The consciousness of the whole country has become colored with lust and yet we talk of moral character. This obsession with lust has become so deeply ingrained that people cannot forget, even for a moment, who is a man and who is a woman; it has become impossible to forget. But it is people like me who talk of such corrupting things; good people do not talk like this. People should be careful. Why is there any need to come to me? There is absolutely no need.

There is also no need to write letters to me, for I

write very disturbing replies. So my third request to you is: please do not write letters to me. With letters from women it becomes a big problem. If I do not reply to their letters, then I get reminders enclosing the first letter. And if I *do* reply, then the problem starts. So please do not write letters to me. Whatever you need to ask me, ask here.

If somebody just has to meet me, then for men it is not so difficult but if a woman wants to meet me, and especially if she is young, then she should bring her father along to act as protector. Older women should bring their husbands along as they will protect them. And if still older, then they should bring their son along, he will be their protector. But never come alone. It is not right to come alone. For I can be very loving!

Himmatbhai Joshi is here; he must be sitting somewhere. His wife, Jassu, went to Indore with me. She was put up in a room next to mine.

In the evening, she came to my room and said: "I'm going to sleep here, in your room."

I told her: "It's a huge room, sleep."

Now it never occurred to me that I was asking a woman to sleep in my room.

Surely there must also be a parliamentarian in Indore. It seems that the parliamentarian in Indore is fast asleep and not concerned about character. That is why people in Indore should not vote for him. He is not a right man, for he should be aware of who sleeps where, who does what. And somebody slept next to a corrupt man like me. How shameful! But I had told the woman it was okay. She slept. She must have been very happy. It was really lucky that no parliamentarian came to know of it, otherwise it would have become a huge problem.

These people are like… Many times you see vultures

flying in the sky; do not conclude from this that the vultures are *in* the sky. They fly in the sky, but their eyes are on the mounds on the ground, seeking rotten pieces of flesh. The flight is in the sky, but eyes are on pieces of flesh, on dirty ground. Just because they fly in the sky does not mean that they are in the sky. Their focus is on the ground, on unclean, dirty places. You are wherever your eyes are. Being in parliament does not make a difference. Where is your sight? But it is not their fault; these poor people are working for the public good. They have to do this for the benefit of the public.

But my request is that there is no need to come near me. And there is no need also to establish any bonds of love with me because I can form a bond of love with anyone. This is wrong; love itself is wrong!

So this was my third request to you. During these three days, whatever questions you may have about anything discussed here, please hand them over in writing, so that on the last day we can take up all your questions and discuss them.

I am very grateful that you have listened to what I had to say, so patiently and so lovingly. Finally, I bow to the godliness present in all of us. Please accept my greetings.

Chapter 2

The Seven Chakras

My beloved ones.

Before we begin our journey within, it is important to become familiar with the path we are going to take. It is necessary to know a little about the doors we will knock on and to understand the locks which will have to be opened.

Travelers who begin their journey without knowing anything about the route are more likely to get lost than to reach their destination. On the outside, at least the roads can be seen, whereas inside there is no visible path. Outside, there are signposts showing where a road goes; within, there are neither signs nor milestones nor land-marks. It is all uncharted territory – there are no maps. Perhaps that is why man strays much more within than he does without. In today's discussion, it will be good to understand a few important points about the path that leads within.

The first important thing to understand is that the physical body we see is only the top layer of numerous bodies. Inside this body there are also other bodies; the body we are aware of is not the only one. And the moment we begin our journey inside, we will need to pass through those layers of bodies. Before we reach our core, we will have to go past all the layers of bodies.

Just below our physical body – the one that can be seen, formed from food – is the etheric body, the life force. It is important to understand a little about this etheric body because we will need to cross it. Passing through something without understanding can lead us astray, can be dangerous and can cause us harm.

As I said, below our physical body is this "electric" body which we call the life force. It is because of this life force that we are aware of our physical body. Even when this body drops, the etheric body remains. Even after death, it survives for a few hours as it is eager to reunite with the physical body.

That is why in societies where people have become aware of this, they burn corpses immediately after death; they do not preserve the dead body. Dead bodies are consigned to the flames due to the deep experiences of the etheric body. As soon as the physical body is burned, the attraction of the life force toward the physical body disappears. Otherwise, the etheric body, together with the soul, will keep wandering around the dead physical body. There is a great possibility of this happening.

The life force that exists just below the physical body is extraordinary. Even before we knew anything about electricity, meditators had already discovered the electric nature of the body. That is the reason why, for thousands of years, meditators have been meditating either on a wooden board or a tiger skin or deer skin. If while passing through the electric body, there is any possibility of the electric life force escaping from the physical body it can cause grave harm, even death. This has been known through experience for a long time.

It is also known that the difference between a man and woman is on account of this electric body. The differences that we see at the level of the physical body are gross; the real, subtle, differences between a man and a woman are at the level of the electric body. Man's life force is the positive terminal; woman's life force is the negative terminal. The electric charge in a man's body is positive, that in a woman's negative. This is the reason for the attraction between the two.

But as soon as a person begins to enter a meditative state, the charge of the life force flowing toward the physical body gradually begins to lose its attraction, its sharpness, its energy, and begins to move inward. The day the life force ceases to flow toward the physical body and flows toward the other layers within, from that moment the person is no longer a mere man or woman. In the consciousness, there is no longer any question of identification with being a man or woman.

Buddha was once meditating for a few days near a mountain. It was night, a full-moon night. A few people from the city had come to the forest and had brought a prostitute with them for some fun, for enjoyment, for pleasure. Totally drunk, they started dancing. They stripped the prostitute of her clothes. When she realized that they were all completely drunk, the naked woman ran away. When the men sobered up they were bewildered; they began to look for the woman, but couldn't find her.

There was no one except Buddha in that forest. He was sitting under a tree, deep in meditation. The men went up to Buddha, shook him and asked: "Monk, you must surely have seen a woman running this way; there are footprints on the road. That woman was naked, a prostitute. We want to ask you in which direction she has she gone."

Buddha replied: "Someone surely ran past me, but it is difficult for me to say whether the person was a man or a woman. If you had come to me ten years ago, I could have told you. But ever since the man in me has withdrawn, I am aware of a woman outside only if I consciously make an effort, not spontaneously. I do not even know if she was wearing any clothes or not. Ever since I became unaware of whether or not there are any clothes on my body, the question of whether or not others are clothed has also disappeared."

Buddha added: "Whatever we see outside is a reflection of who we are. But I ask you, friends, why are you looking for her? Would it not be far better if on this quiet, full-moon night you try and find yourself?"

No one knows whether they heard him or not. It is said – people are always saying – seek yourself. But who listens? We are all running to find someone else. This search for the other – if we understand it correctly – is a search by the body that is the life force. The life-force body is incomplete; it has either the positive charge or the negative charge. It is constantly seeking the other which will make it complete. By itself it is incomplete, only half. The half-body seeks the other half, desires the missing half. That is why the search for the other continues.

The electric body layer within us is joined with our physical body at seven points. At seven places there is a contact field, a point of contact and these seven locations are known as chakras. The electric body touches the physical body, is in contact with it, at seven different places. And it is from these seven points, from the layer that is the charged body, that our physical body gets the power, the life energy, the life force.

It is important to understand a little about these seven chakras because as soon as a person begins to enter a meditative state – as soon as the inner journey begins – he has to pass near these seven chakras. Knowingly or unknowingly, he will have to pass by them. Every person's experience will be a little different because for every person usually a different chakra will be active.

It is also vital to know about these chakras because it will help you a great deal in gaining an insight into your personality, in understanding yourself. You will be able to understand what kind of a person you are, what your nature is, and with this understanding it is easier to go within. Once we understand what kind of a person we are, then we also know where we are at present. We have to begin our journey from where we are. How can a person who does not even know where he stands begin his journey? It is not enough to know where we want to go, it is even more important to know where we are at present. In order to reach where we want to go, we will need to start from where we are.

These seven chakras are extraordinary elements, the most mysterious components in a person's body. They cannot be found by cutting open the body. That is why a physiologist will say: "What chakras? Where are the chakras? The body does not have any chakras." The physical body certainly does not have any chakras. *Chakras* refer to the other body inside, the life force which touches the physical body at seven locations. It is through these seven doors that this physical body gets its energy, its life.

The first chakra is located at the lower end of the spine, at the back of the body, at the base. This is an extraordinary chakra. We will find out something about this one. The first chakra is there and the last chakra is on the top of the head. In between these there are five other chakras. The second is near the genitals, next to the sex organs. It is this chakra that is responsible for the sex urge which influences and activates sexual feelings.

In every part of the world, as soon as a person becomes even a little conscious the first thing he tries to do is to cover his genitals, because this chakra is such that if another person were to look at it directly, with a firm gaze, he would be able to influence it. That is why man has no problem in baring all the other parts of the body, but finds it essential to cover this most important chakra – whether with leaves, with clothes, or in some other manner.

The second chakra, which we call the sex center, or the sex chakra, is the most active within a person because nature has maximum need of this. It is through this chakra that the body is reborn, reproduces itself. It is through this that mankind is filled with the urge and desire to reproduce. The entire process of giving birth to life is due to this chakra.

However, a person who lives only under the influence of this chakra, in whom this chakra is most active, finds his life obsessed with sex, there is nothing but lust in his life. He may accumulate money, or fame, or reach positions of power, but money, fame, and power will remain for him just a means of satisfying his lust, for sexual gratification. His entire life will be centered around this.

I was reading the biography of a very well-known writer, a great novelist – Anatole France. Toward the end of his life, Anatole said to one of his friends… His friend had asked him what he considered most important in his life. Anatole replied: "I will tell you something that I have not mentioned to anyone else: the most significant thing in my life was lust, sex."

The friend was taken aback. He responded: "You are such a great novelist, such a well-known writer. I always thought that in your life literature, art, music would be most vital."

He replied: "They were all secondary, merely cover-ups."

If we wish to know our personality more deeply, then we first need to investigate what the center of our person is, where we actually live. It is this core of our persona that will indicate to us which chakra is the most active and most important in our body. Also keep in mind that it's only through whichever chakra is the most significant that we see and understand our entire life; we will not be able to understand anything apart from it.

In Khajuraho there are sculptures. A well-known artist from America came to see them. One of my friends was the education minister of Vindhya Pradesh and the central government had instructed him to show these sculptures to the American artist. This friend was very nervous because there are so many nude statues, so many obscene sculptures there. The American artist would be flabbergasted. What would he think of Indian culture? What would he think of our people? And such offensive statues have been discovered on temples – statues showing sexual intercourse.

He was very tense, but there was no way out; the orders had come from above. So this friend had to go along with the American artist to Khajuraho. With great trepidation, with fear in his heart, he showed him all the sculptures, dreading all the time that he might ask: "Are these sculptures really representative of your culture? These are your temples – you who call yourself spiritual?"

But that artist was so absorbed in the sculptures that he said not a word. The friend, however, kept repeating that the statues do not represent our culture, do not symbolize our basic traditions; that some misguided people had built these temples under the wrong influence.

When they came out the artist thanked my friend profusely. My friend was however still very edgy. He said: "When you return to America, please do not tell anyone that in India we have temples with such obscene statues."

The man responded: "Obscene statues! What are you saying? I will have to go back and see them again. I have never seen such beautiful sculptures, never seen such divine images."

Then he added: "Let us go back there, because you are more knowledgeable than me. If you say the statues are obscene, then I will have to go back again because what I have seen just now... I have never seen such divine figures before."

We see only what we are capable of seeing. We do not see what is. What we are able to see is all that we *can* see; all that we see in life is really our own projection. We see outside whatever is within us. For a man filled with lust, every object in the world seems to be full of lust. For a man filled with godliness, the whole world appears to be filled with the divine. To a man filled with anger, every person will appear to be angry. For a lover, the whole world will appear to be flowing with love. We see what we are.

This whole external world is only a projection of what we are within. The world is like a screen on which we see all that is hidden inside us. So if a person visualizes only sex and passion all around him, then he should understand that the sex center is the most active in his personality. It is so because nature needs it to be so. Nature does not need any other center as much as it needs your sex center; it is only through this that new life can be created.

In animals, there is only life in this center; none of the other centers are active. In most men too, only this center is active, but other centers can also be energized. And keep in mind that as long as only the sex center is active, there is no qualitative difference between us and animals. There is a potential difference: our other centers can become alive and active – but they are not.

Normally man lives only there. Go through the history of mankind and you will find that ninety-nine percent of all literature revolves around lust, around sex. This is amazing! Look at any painting, pick out any statue, watch any film, read any poetry and you will wonder why ninety-nine percent of all of man's energy revolves around sex. Surely there has to be a reason.

The sex center is the only center that is fully active. And remember: when practicing celibacy, there are techniques to make the sex center inactive. As it becomes inactive, thoughts of passion and sex vanish from a person's life as if they had never been there. It's just like switching off a lamp. When it is switched off, the light disappears as if it had never been there because the contact is broken at the point from where the current was flowing. The practice of celibacy does not mean that someone has just to sit with closed eyes: the main scientific principle behind celibacy is to make the sex center inactive and there are ways, methods, and techniques to achieve this.

Hundreds of years ago, young men up to the age of twenty-five were trained in the practice of celibacy. The reason for this was not that at the time there were no films for them to watch. The reason was also not that men could not see women or women could not see men. The reason was also not that they had taken a vow – there were no reasons of this sort. There was a scientific basis for such a practice. That center can be made dormant, and as soon as it becomes inactive the sex urge vanishes. One is not even aware of it until the center is re-opened and awakened again.

Approximately three out of a hundred people are born with their sex center weak or passive. Hence this three percent of people cannot understand what all the fuss is about. Why are people so mad? Why are they so obsessed? It is totally beyond their understanding, beyond their imagination.

In small children, the sex center is not active. Gradually it begins to come alive. By the time they are fourteen years of age it is fully energized; before that they are not aware it. Only when the center becomes active do they become aware of their sexual urges. If the center is not active, the awareness cannot be there.

In your consciousness, it should become absolutely clear whether or not this center is overly active. If it is predominantly active, then before and after meditation you must repeat in your mind that this center should become less active. Before meditation and after meditation, bring your attention to this center and suggest to your mind that this center should become less vigorous. After a few days, you will notice a qualitative change beginning to take place.

Above this center is the third center – the *manipura* chakra, the one at the navel. This is the center of fear and apprehension. Just as the genitals react at the sex center, you may have observed that whenever you are over-whelmed by fear, there is a peculiar feeling, a disturbing sensation, near your navel – at the *manipura*, the center for fear.

If you are driving a car and have a sudden accident, the shock that you feel in the body will be at the navel, not anywhere else. If a man suddenly jumps on your chest with a dagger, again the biggest shock will be felt in this area. The area around the navel forms the center for fear. That is why in extreme cases of fear a person can also lose control over his bowels and bladder; there is no other reason for this. The *manipura* chakra, the fear center, becomes so active that it becomes necessary to empty the stomach; otherwise it cannot be fully active.

It is very important for people whose fear center is very active to be more aware of their *manipura*. This is the reason why, in ancient times, when people were being trained for warfare there was great focus on strengthening the area around the navel. Fear is felt there. It does not attach itself anywhere else. Fear will never overcome you in the head. Whenever fear over-comes you, it will be in the stomach region. Women are more often prone to fear. The sole reason for this is that inside their stomachs women have the womb where the fetus grows, and because of this the area around the *manipura* gradually becomes weaker and weaker.

As far as fear is concerned, there is no other difference between men and women. Because women in the West refuse to produce children, their fear goes on reducing. If women were to refuse to produce children altogether, their condition would be almost similar to that of men. This is why, all over the world, in societies where women are trying to be like men, they are refusing motherhood. It is not possible to become a man as long as the process of being a mother is still functioning. The possibility of becoming a mother fills the entire personality with fear. The *manipura* chakra is the center of fear.

When you are afraid, your digestion will be disturbed. Worry upsets digestion – worry and fear. There is a lot of anxiety and fear in the world today. There is no other reason for the disease of ulcers. The systems in the stomach, the entire digestive system, will progressively deteriorate and be in a state of disorder the more a person is afraid, worried, and anxious. It is important to remember that those whose sex center is vigorous will follow a tradition or religion that is in some way governed by sexual indulgence. The symbols of the most ancient religions are sexual, phallic, in nature, like the *shivalinga* of Shankar. In Greece, Rome, Egypt, Mesopotamia, or in Mohenjodaro, the most ancient sculptures and images are all phallic in nature, symbols of the sexual organs. It appears that twenty thousand years ago, when civilization had not developed very much beyond that of animals, even the supreme power was represented by sexual symbols. This was the center that was the most active, most alive.

As man evolved a little more and went beyond this center, beyond lust, and when he started to think of other things, a new image of the supreme power formed: a power to be afraid of. In the Old Testament, as in many other ancient religious scriptures, images of this supreme power are such that they generate terror, fear. It seems as if man's second center, the center of fear, gave rise to a supreme power that arouses terror.

If the man praying in the temple with hands folded – the man bowing his head at the supreme power's feet, trembling and pleading "O God, please save me!" – pays even a little attention, he will realize that at the moment of praying his *manipura* chakra is the most alive. As the world becomes more educated, as the fear element recedes, religions based mainly on prayer and supplication will gradually begin to vanish because those religions were formed and developed from the *manipura* chakra. If this center is strengthened, they will disappear.

More women than men visit the temples. There is no reason for this except that women have a weaker *manipura* than men. For every man you see in the temples, there will be four women. All temples function because of women; all the sages and saints are there because of women. The supreme power that generates fear appeals to them, seems meaningful to them.

For a man whose life is filled with fear, it is necessary that he carefully try a few experiments at his *manipura* chakra. In order to strengthen this chakra some suggestions have to be given in that direction. And it is amazing: as these centers are life-centers – centers carrying electric charges – they can be transformed by mere suggestion. Nothing else needs to be done.

Next, the fourth center, the heart center or the heart chakra. This is the center of craving, the center of attachment, the center of desire. People who are under the influence of this center will, in some form or other, be initiated into a religion that is governed by devotion, a religion where one can become possessed by attachment and desire. It is important to also understand this chakra. It is vital to appreciate what this center is capable of doing, for this center is also active.

In the East it is very active; in the Western countries less so. This is the reason why the family structure in the West is beginning to fall apart. The breaking up of families in the West cannot be stopped until a scientific way is evolved to strengthen their heart chakra. Families will go on breaking up there because the center of attachment has broken down – or is starting to break down – and has become weak and inactive. Even in the countries of the East this has started to happen.

It must also be remembered that this center is more active in women than in men. That is why the person who creates the family is not the man but the woman. Do not be under the misconception that man has created the institution of family. Man cannot create a family. In fact, the family exists in spite of man; man is always looking for ways to escape from the family, he wants to run away. His center of attachment is not so powerful.

The entire civilization has been developed by the woman. Family and home are her creations. From the beginning, man has been a gypsy; he has always been a wanderer. He wanders and is happy; the more he drifts the happier he will be. The woman wants to tie herself to one place and settle down. She finds wandering very difficult as it is not what her heart desires. She needs to form an attachment – a small piece of land, a small home where she can settle down. That is why a family, any type of family, never has a man at its center, he is always at the periphery; the center is always the woman. It is essential to focus on this center of attachment to understand whether it is dominant in your personality or not.

Here I am just explaining the role of these centers. Later we will explore how we can use them in other ways. After this center comes the throat center. This chakra is the source of speech and thought within a person. People in whom this center is dominant often spend their lives in discussion and contemplation. They are not able to do anything else. The practice of observing silence is a technique for making the throat center less powerful, less dominant.

Then comes what I had mentioned to you yesterday when speaking about our meditation: between the eyes is the sixth center – the third-eye chakra. This is a very important chakra as it is through this chakra that a man transforms or can transform his entire personality. But our third-eye chakra is so weak that we are not even able to give ourselves any instructions.

A man may decide at night to get up at four in the morning. At four o'clock the next morning he finds himself saying: "Not today, it is too cold, we will see tomorrow." When he gets up later that morning, he repents and says: "I myself had decided to get up at four in the morning. What happened? I promise that I will definitely get up tomorrow; I will not forget." Night comes, and at four in the morning he again finds himself saying: "No, not today, I will see tomorrow." In the morning he again repents. What is happening? A man promises himself something and does not fulfill it. He decides to do something and is not able to do it. What is the reason behind all this? There is only one reason: our third-eye chakra

– the center of our will, responsible for our resolve – is very weak, very inactive, almost nonexistent.

I said yesterday that while meditating your attention should be on the spot between the two eyes – on that center. When your attention is focused there, whatever you decide to do will enter your consciousness firmly and deeply. If the focus is kept precisely there, you will be able to do whatever you set your mind to. You may have noticed that whenever you have to decide something, or come to a conclusion, then the maximum pressure is felt between the eyes. When a major decision has to be taken, when you have to decide what you should do, then you will feel pressure exactly where I am telling you: at the spot between the two eyes. All decisions are taken from there, all directives come from there, all resolves are made there. A person who is able to make resolves from this center will find that his resolves are put into practice, the decisions taken here are carried out, and the transformation that he wants to make to his personality begins to take effect.

It is very strange: in order to bring about a change in our personality, it is not so much a question of our putting in an effort as it is of our resolve. Determination is the secret to the transformation of our personality, not work. But the resolve should be total and total resolve does not originate from any other part of the body than the third-eye chakra. That is why all practices of meditation are centered in or around the third-eye chakra, because it is from there that it is possible to enter a meditative state and go deep within.

If you were to ask a certain question of the African tribesmen, or the Australian bushmen, or the aboriginal tribes living in the forests of the Amazonas, you would be surprised at their answer. When these tribals heard for the first time that people in other parts of the world think with their heads, they could not stop laughing. They said: "No one can think from the head, we think from our stomachs." The tribal man does indeed think from his stomach. He thinks from the navel, from the *manipura* chakra. They have not developed much beyond a primitive state.

For thousands of years, millions of people have believed that the process of thinking happens in the belly – in the stomach – not in the head. Even among us there are very few who think from their heads. Believers always think from their bellies, never from their heads, because for believing there is no need for thought. Therefore, for a person who is a believer, the chakras at the higher levels never develop; only the lower level chakras are activated.

This is why I keep protesting against blind faith in anyone, because until the time that a person begins to think for himself, his higher chakras responsible for thought will never develop. If those chakras are not developed, then a person becomes almost like a leaf that is blown here and there by the wind. He doesn't possess anything of his own: any will, any resolve, any stability. He is just following someone. No one else causes as much harm to man as politicians do. All the politicians in the world give orders and tell you that you just need to obey them. Religious leaders give instructions and tell people that they have to follow them. Your third-eye chakra never gets a chance to develop.

Mankind seems to be in a wretched state and the main reason for this sorry state is that mankind is just being given directives, has never been given a chance to develop its own thinking. We start early by giving instructions to little children – do this, don't do that. We never worry about the development of their thought process, their decision making, their judgment. In those children the third-eye chakra never matures, it remains incomplete, and if a person's third-eye chakra is not developed, his personality cannot mature.

We keep on urging children to become this, become that, forgetting that they will never be able to become either. They *are* able to, but in order to do so, they need to pay attention to those chakras which are responsible for transforming and developing the personality. Parents who know, teachers who know, will put all their efforts into developing the third-eye chakra. Today's education is very deficient, meaningless, because it is not based on the exploration of any fundamental truths about man; no thought is given to this.

If we are able to develop the third-eye chakra of chil dren, build up their resolve by the time they go to university, we can transform the whole world. A new world, a new man will be born. A man who has power; a man who does what he thinks, *can* do what he thinks – a man of courage, a man who is bold and valiant. But it is not possible for us because in us the chakra from where all these qualities emerge is dormant, inactive.

Gurdjieff, who died several years ago, was an extraordinary man. He used to try a small experiment with his meditators. The name of the experiment was the "Stop Exercise" where he would ask his students to just stop what they were doing. We are sitting here. If Gurdjieff were to do his experiment here, he would say: "When I say 'Stop!' then everyone stop and freeze the way you are. If you have opened your mouth to say something, then do not close your mouth, leave it open.

If you have raised a foot to walk, then do not move, leave your foot raised, irrespective of whether you fall or die." Why? What kind of insane exercise is this? What is the meaning of it? But the people who did this experiment with Gurdjieff were transformed. They said that they were astonished that such a simple experiment could bring about such a radical change.

A lot of courage is required to do this. You will try to deceive yourself: "Is somebody looking at me? My foot is too high and aching; let me lower it a little." If you lower your foot and put it down, you have not harmed anyone, but the chakra within – to develop which the exercise was being done – will remain as it is, and the exercise will have become meaningless. But if you maintain your resolve and keep your position as you were: eyes open if they were open, no blinking; hand up, if it was up; mouth open, if it was open; one leg raised, if it was raised; waist bent, if it was bent, no movement... Yes, it will be very painful, but whoever does this is giving himself an order, is strengthening his will and resolve.

Gurdjieff was once staying in Tbilisi, then a city in Russia, with thirty of his friends. He had taken them there for meditation. He had instructed them that for thirty days continuously they would be doing nothing but the stop exercise. "Whenever I shout 'Stop!' you have to stop wherever you are. If somebody is having a bath, he stops there; if someone is eating, he stops there. Whatever you are doing, you have to freeze, as if you have become a statue."

Nearby, next to where they had set up their tents, was a stream. The stream was generally dry and only occasionally water was released into it. In the morning, all thirty of them were strolling nearby. Three of them were crossing the stream. It was dry, no water in it. Suddenly from inside his tent Gurdjieff shouted: "Stop!" Everyone froze, including the three men.

At that moment, Gurdjieff was still inside his tent, somebody released the water, and the water came flooding into the stream. The water rose up to the three men's waists, then up to their necks. When the water began rising even above their necks, one of the men jumped out of the stream. He said: "He does not know what is happening. He is sitting inside his tent, and here our lives are threatened" – and he jumped out.

He did not realize that he had missed an opportunity. When his whole body was urging him to jump out, his resolve could have said: "No, I will not move! I am willing to put my life at stake, I will not waver." The chakra which so far had been lying dormant could have awakened. One shock, one jolt, and it would have started. But he missed the opportunity; he jumped out. Most people would jump out. Even you might have jumped out if you had been in his place. It was not a mistake.

Now two men were left. The water came up to their mouths. When it rose up to their noses, the second man thought it now too dangerous and jumped out of the stream. But the third man stood firm. He was not blind; he could see the danger. His life was at stake; death was staring him in the face. The water rose above his head. But he said to himself: "Now let whatever happens, happen. I am determined; so be it."

Gurdjieff ran out of his tent like a man possessed. The water had been released into the stream intentionally. He jumped into the water and pulled the man out. The man had been transformed. Gurdjieff said: "The opportunity came, and two of your colleagues missed it. But even under so much pressure, when death itself was staring you in the face, *your* resolve did not waver."

What else was needed for the chakra to awaken? It came alive. This man had been transformed. Now whatever this man wishes will happen. If he tells his thoughts to stop, then thoughts cannot move within him. If he instructs his breath to stop, the breath will not come again. If he tells himself that he will drop dead this moment, you will find that he dies. Now whatever this man wants for himself will happen.

About three hundred years ago, in South India, the sixtieth birthday of a noted musician was being celebrated with great pomp. He had a lot of eminent friends, a lot of well-known students, and he knew a lot of renowned kings and princes. All of them had come together and made the arrangements for the celebration. Thousands of his students had come bringing gifts.

A poor mendicant, who earned his living by playing a stringed instrument on the streets and begging, was also his student. He had nothing with him. Half the night was over, and people were leaving after giving their gifts.

The beggar went up to the door and said to the guard: "Let me go inside; I too want to give a gift to my teacher."

But the guards saw that his hands were empty, his clothes were in tatters. The guard said: "I do not see anything with you."

The man replied: "But *I* am here."

The guard thought he was a little mad, but decided to let him go in.

He went in. All the people were on their way out; the whole house was adorned with gifts worth millions of rupees. The beggar went up to his guru, bowed his head to his feet, and said: "I too bring you a gift. Will you accept it?"

The teacher also saw that there was nothing in his hands. He said: "But I do not see any gift."

The beggar replied: "*I* am here." With folded hands he prayed: "O divine power, I have nothing else to give to my guru. Let my life be my gift."

With these words his breath stopped – and he dropped dead.

What kind of a man was this? He just uttered the words "*My life…*"

How many times have you said the Hindi blessing "*Meri umur aapko mil jaye* – may my years be added to your life"? It will not happen. You know it, and so does the other. But if your third-eye chakra is activated, then you do not say such a thing, even by mistake. It is said that saints never say anything bad about anyone. The reason for this is not that they cannot say such things. They could say negative things, but it would be dangerous. Anything that comes from someone with such resolve can become true. A thought coming from a person with great determination is very alive. It carries an exceptional energy, a unique power.

We often say to people that the mind does not remain quiet. We try a lot of things, a lot of techniques, but the mind remains disturbed, ever active. It will always be so because you are not aware that you can instruct the mind to stop – and it will have to stop. Of course, this stop needs to come with considerable energy.

I have heard an incident about Jesus…

Jesus, along with two friends, was in a boat on a lake. Suddenly, a violent storm came up. Jesus was sleeping in a corner. His friends shook him and said: "The boat is about to sink, there is danger, and you are still sleeping."

Jesus replied: "Let me sleep a little more. I was up late last night and am tired. If there is danger, you deal with it."

But the boat was now on the verge of sinking any moment. The friends came again, they were angry. Here they were, about to die, about to drown, and this man continued to sleep.

They woke Jesus up. Jesus said: "Go and tell the lake to calm down."

They replied: "Are you mad? Can a lake obey anyone?"

Jesus said: "If the waters inside you obey you, then the waters outside will also do so."

If you don't have any faith, any belief, in the lake inside you, what can you say to the lakes outside? The story is beautiful.

Jesus spoke to the lake and said: "Be silent, calm down."

And it is said that the lake became calm, the storm vanished.

Whether or not the lake outside became calm or not isn't the question. But I can assure you about the lake inside. If once a resolve is developed within, you turn inside and say "Enough," then a deep silence will spread inside you, as if there was no turbulence, never had been.

But all the time we keep crying, screaming: practice

tolerance, pray, recite holy mantras! – and various other things. Nothing happens; nothing will. But it can happen by activating just one chakra, by developing your will and resolve. But that does not happen, we don't do it. Then we claim that nothing is working, nothing is happening. Whatever we want, it cannot happen from anywhere except from this chakra.

That is why during meditation we need to keep a special focus on this chakra. And it is amazing that the sharper our focus on this chakra, the sooner it becomes awakened. The secret to activating the chakra is to keep our attention on it, our focus on it. The chakra that becomes our focus will be the one that becomes active.

You may not be aware that if you place your fingers on your pulse and count the number of beats, and then count them again a second time with all your attention on the pulse, you will find that the number of beats has increased. Just a little more attention and the speed has increased. Sit down and focus all your attention on your breath, and you will find that the breathing becomes deeper.

In the case of chakras it is even stranger: which-ever chakra you focus on gets activated. Attention is the food for chakras, their fuel. It's like filling up a car with petrol. Then it is ready to move; it cannot move by just saying the word *petrol*. Although I *have* heard one such anecdote!

It happened…

Once a man walked into a Ford showroom to buy a car. The manager drove out the car that the customer liked for a trial run. After going for just seven miles the car suddenly shuddered to a stop. The customer was very surprised and said: "It is very strange that the car has suddenly stopped after going for a mere seven miles. This will not do."

The manager asked his driver: "Please check. Did you fill the car up with petrol, or did you drive it out without doing so?"

The driver replied: "I totally forgot to put in any petrol. It's a brand new car. There is no petrol in it, never has been."

The customer was surprised and asked: "Then how did it run for seven miles?"

The manager responded: "It can run this far just on the name Ford."

Maybe cars can function like this, but mere names will not do for chakras. Here something else needs to be done. They need fuel and only one type of fuel. In the world of consciousness, the sole fuel, the only power, is total focus. That is why I said that while rapidly asking "Who am I?" all your attention should be on the third-eye chakra – then you will experience it.

Today for fifteen minutes we will try this. Before doing our experiment, touch the top of your head with your hands. After fifteen minutes of the experiment, do it again. You will notice that the top of your head has become warm, while the area around it is not so warm. When something happens inside, its heat permeates outside too. In fact, those who are knowledgeable about chakras can tell you by merely touching your body which of your chakras are active.

Ramakrishna had a strange habit. When Vivekananda went to him for the first time, Ramakrishna took him into the next room, shut the door and said: "Take off your shirt!"

Vivekananda was taken aback, wondering what was happening. Why should he remove his shirt? It was fortunate that he was a man; had he been a woman there would have been a huge problem. Ramakrishna insisted: "First take off your shirt!"

Vivekananda removed his shirt. Ramakrishna placed his hand on his chest and said: "It's fine, it can happen."

Later, Vivekananda asked him, "What did you mean? What can happen? What did you see?"

Ramakrishna replied: "I had to find out which chakra was active in you, otherwise I might have labored in the wrong direction and all my efforts would have been wasted."

This is entirely possible. Why is it possible? It is really quite simple: as soon as a chakra becomes energized – a specific point in the body is awakened – it acquires a different meaning, has a different kind of heat.

In all the images of Buddha or Mahavira, you will have noticed what appears to be locks of hair tied up in huge knots on the top of their heads. These are not locks of hair, but symbols of the final chakra, indicating that it has been activated. The final chakra has been awakened and these "locks" symbolize it. You will also never have seen a beard or mustache on Buddha or Mahavira; they are not there. Similarly, on their heads it is not hair; it is just a symbol. If you count the locks of hair, you will note that the count goes to exactly one thousand. This count of thousand is nothing else than the one thousand petals of the lotus – symbolic of the final chakra.

This final chakra is located on the top of the head. Any person in whom this chakra is energized can be recognized merely by touching the top of his head. A slight bulge will appear there, a slight projection apart from the rest of the head. This final chakra is the *sahasrar* chakra, the seventh center. It comes after the third-eye chakra, and it is through the third-eye chakra that it is possible to enter the *sahasrar* chakra. When this chakra is activated, a person is able to distance himself from his physical body. It is then that he realizes that he is not the body; he is something else.

These are the seven chakras. Why have I spoken about them? I have talked about them so that you may be aware of your primary chakra. Firstly, with complete understanding, you have to know your primary chakra. Then you have to make the effort to progress to the higher level chakras. Maximum effort and attention is needed on the third-eye chakra because without this no progress is possible on the path of spiritual development.

Keep in mind also that the chakras below the navel are not only positioned there but are also the lower chakras. The chakras above the navel are not only higher in the body, they also further the higher growth of your personality. The higher the active chakra, the greater is the person's development, and the final chakra is proof of ultimate growth. As soon as you meditate on "Who am I?" with great energy, within a period of three to four months you will begin to clearly see and experience your chakras. You will be able to see which of your chakras are alive and which are dormant and you will also realize that depending on which chakras are active, their characteristics of attraction, repulsion, anger, or desire are all alive in you.

If a person therefore wants to put a stop to his anger or attachment – remember, no one can just stop anger and attachment – it's only by making his chakra inactive that the transformation begins to happen. If he wishes to awaken love it cannot be done, but give energy to the chakra of love and love begins to flow. Building resolve also cannot be done just like that. No matter how much he might say "I will not fear darkness, I will not be afraid of my enemies," nothing will happen. He will still be afraid of the dark; he will still fear his enemy. The one who says "I will not be afraid" is showing proof of his fear, confirming that he is afraid. No brave man ever says "I do not know fear." Anyone who says that he does not know fear, for certain cannot be brave. Otherwise even the thought of not being afraid would not arise in him.

Two young Rajput lads came to Akbar's court one morning. They were twins. Standing in Akbar's court they said: "We wish to enroll in your army. We are both very brave. Do you have any need of us?"

Akbar replied: "You call yourself brave lads, but do you have any certificates, any proof of your bravery? How can we believe that you are brave?"

They both started laughing and said: "We did not expect that a person like you would raise such a question. Can there ever be a certificate for bravery? Can there be any proof? And who should a brave man go to for such a certificate? If a man were to bring such a certificate, then that in itself would be proof that the man is not brave. Will a brave man go to another and ask him for a certificate saying he is brave? Will a man of character go to another and ask him to confirm in writing that he is a man of character? If character itself is not proof, then what letter, what certificate, can be proof?"

They then added: "We are brave; this much we can

say. If we get an opportunity, we can show you our bravery. But we do not have any certificates."

Akbar responded: "Then how can we see your bravery? How can we know?"

The boys asked: "You really want to see?"

Akbar replied: "Yes, I do."

In a flash, both of them pulled out their swords. For a moment Akbar was stunned, wondering what their intention was. Then the swords clashed and the duel began. The twins were courageous and brave lads. Their flowering into youth had barely begun. With their sharp swords they pierced each other's chests. In a moment, both of them were on the ground with blood spurting out of their bodies.

Akbar cried: "Fools, what have you done?"

They said: "Except for being willing to die, what other proof can a brave man give? What other proof of bravery can there be except that we can even meet death with laughter? Death to us is a game."

Akbar immediately called his Rajput chiefs and asked: "What is this? What has happened?"

They said: "It was your mistake; you do not know that you should never question a Rajput's bravery. Henceforth, do not ever ask this question again, even inadvertently because there is only one answer: we consider death to be a game."

These two young boys... You can imagine how energized their third-eye chakra must have been. If they could play with death like that, then they could also reach the ultimate reality in the same manner.

Keep in mind that on the path to the ultimate reality one needs to be a warrior. It is not a path that can be taken by a trader – it is not. It is the road for a man of resolve, a man of courage. That is why, as bravery and valor have become less in the world, our bond with the ultimate reality has continued to weaken. The world today is ruled by monks and businessmen. We can safely say that the twentieth century is the century of traders. If anyone is powerful today it is the cunning shopkeeper.

If we look at our history, we will find that in the beginning we were influenced by a different class of people. Now another kind is powerful; tomorrow perhaps yet another kind will be influential. But one thing is certain: the less the courage in any society, the less the resolve will be; the less the resolve, the less the spiritual progress will be because, fundamentally, spiritual progress is essentially the outcome of resolve.

That is why my emphasis is on this chakra; this is the door. So today when we sit for meditation, bring all your power, all your energy to the spot between the eyes; something should begin happening there, a small sun orbiting. When all your attention is there, within a few days – it can happen today too – your experience will be as if a small sun has started its orbit within and the warmth of it is spreading all over your forehead: a miniature sun orbiting rapidly.

The orbiting miniature sun will seem as the real sun would appear if you looked at it through a cone formed by your hands. As your meditation becomes deeper, the sun will increase in size. And as the size increases, you will observe a change beginning to take place in your personality, a change from what you were yesterday. You acquire a new power: a spine is formed, the feet have greater stability, your resolve is more potent. It is with this resolve, through the door of this resolve, that man enters the temple of the ultimate reality.

We will talk more about this temple tomorrow. Now we will sit for our meditation. Remember it is not enough to just sit, and also remember that repeating the question softly is not enough. Keep in mind that there are many people here. If all these people are making a collective effort to meditate, then your effort is not solitary – you will share the fruit of their efforts. Tomorrow, I will talk about how this benefit accumulates.

If two thousand people are sitting together and meditating, then the collective thought and resolve of two thousand people creates a current of air, a psychic atmosphere. Waves of these thoughts rise swiftly; they will reach and touch your forehead. Thoughts are not only present within you; their motions, their waves begin to spread all around you. But in India, collective praying has never been developed. In all forms of religion practiced in India, a basic weakness has been that not one of them has encouraged or developed collective prayer.

Collective meditation has an amazing significance. What a single individual cannot do, can easily be done by people acting in concert. Therefore, please do not let this opportunity go to waste by merely sitting here. You can sit by yourself too, at home, but this is a unique opportunity; two thousand people are with you.

You may not realize that if you are running alone, it is one thing; if two thousand people are running with you – their hands touching yours, their feet scraping yours, their voices in your ears – it is quite another experience. I have even heard that in the military, generals forbid their troops to march in time when crossing a bridge. The reason is that if the feet step in unison, there is a danger of the bridge collapsing. They order the troops to march out of rhythm, break the rhythm, so that their feet fall at random. If a thousand people cross a bridge, their feet hitting simultaneously, then the pattern that is created – the sound that emerges, the wave that is formed – can easily destroy the bridge.

You may also not know that if a tamboura is lying in the corner of a room, and nearby ten similar instruments are played in identical rhythm, there is every possibility that the strings of that tamboura will begin resonating in exactly the same manner, producing identical sounds, as the other ten tambouras. This is possible.

If two thousand people are sitting here and meditating on one thought, focusing on one resolve, then even the heartbeat of a man who is sitting in their midst increases. His resolve strengthens, his consciousness is also struck by the winds coming from all directions, by the waves touching him from all sides. I will also speak about how this happens tomorrow. But if we do this with vigor, with all our power, there is no reason for it not to happen.

Yesterday I explained the meditation to you already, but for the benefit of new friends who may have come today, I will take two minutes to explain again. First, you have to sit down and straighten your spine. The five fingers of one hand are to be interlocked with the five fingers of the other hand and put in your lap. The interlocked fingers have to be closed to form a fist because the greater the force with which you ask yourself the question, the tighter your fist will become. This will be the proof of how forcefully you are asking yourself the question. The spine is straight. Then you have to close your eyes and after shutting your eyes, the lips are to be closed. The tongue will be in contact with the roof of your mouth, lips tightly closed.

Now, with all your strength, you have to ask yourself "Who am I? Who am I?" The question has to be asked rapidly, so that there is no space left between two consecutive "Who am I's." It has to be asked with such rapidity that there is absolutely no energy left anywhere inside. With all your power you have to ask "Who am I?" Your entire being should be shaken, the lake of your life force should be in turmoil. Every pore of your body should ask, every beat of your heart should ask, every breath you take should ask, your entire body should ask "Who am I?" A fever should envelop and engulf your entire being.

Chapter 3

Resolve Is the Key to Awakening

My beloved ones.

I once went into a garden. The garden had only one type of soil; there was only one sky above it. The rays of just one sun fell on it and the same winds used to pass over all of it. The rain that poured down was the same all over the garden and there was just one gardener. Yet the flowers that grew in that garden were all different. I was deeply perplexed. Perhaps at some time, in some other garden, you might have been similarly confused.

The earth is the same, the sky is the same, the sun-rays are the same, the winds are the same, the rains are the same, and the gardener is the same. But the rose bushes grow pink flowers, and the jasmine white flowers; their scent is different. How do the different varieties of flowers manage to draw different colors, different fragrances, different shapes out of the same earth, the same sky and the same sunrays?

I asked the gardener. He answered: "Everything is the same, but the seeds are all different." Such a small seed – what could it possibly extract? A tiny seed, and yet it can ignore such a huge earth, such a vast sky, great winds, put them all aside and extract from them the color of its own choice. A small seed sets aside the vast world and draws from it the fragrance it chooses. How great is the resolve of a tiny seed, greater than the earth, greater than the sky. The seed becomes what it wishes to be. What can there possibly be inside such a tiny seed?

Every seed has its own desire, own will, own resolve. The tiny seed takes only what it needs and leaves everything else untouched. Right next to each other, the rose becomes a rose, the jasmine a jasmine. The rose and the jasmine have a different fragrance; everything is different about them. From the same soil both have drawn their own nourishment.

There are infinite possibilities in life, but we become only that which we absorb from those possibilities. There is an infinite number of ideas and thoughts – subtle variations of these permeate the world – but only for those thoughts for which we have an internal receptivity do we feel an attraction. We are drawn to them like a magnet.

In this world, one man became a Buddha. In this world, one man became a Jesus, another became a Krishna. We live in the same world as they did, but we die and disappear as nobodies. The world from which everything is drawn is exactly the same for everyone – the same sky, earth, winds, the same sun and stars. Everything is the same, so how does every human being become different? Our looks are similar, our bodies appear to be similar, our flesh and bones are similar. Where does the difference happen? Where and when do the personalities begin to differ? How does one man become a Buddha? How does another man get trapped in darkness? How does yet another man get enlightened?

It is important to understand what I spoke about yesterday. I explained that man's persona has seven centers, seven chakras, and from all sides the center that is activated pulls in what is amenable to it. The center becomes receptive. If the center for anger is activated, it will draw in waves of anger from all around it. If the center for love is activated, from all directions it will attract toward itself waves of love. If the center for passion is energized, from all sides waves of lust and passion will race toward it. A man becomes like a deep abyss and from everywhere all that he craves flows into it.

Existence gives each of us what we wish for. So never, even by mistake, complain that you have been given something that you didn't want. Never has anyone got something he did not wish for. The problem is that we are not even aware of what we want. In a state of deep unawareness, we keep wishing for things, and whatever we wish for keeps happening – then we seek someone to blame.

If the jasmine seed complains to existence that it has been given white flowers when it desperately wanted red flowers, then that jasmine seed is in the wrong; that seed had never wished for red flowers. Whatever we are is the result of our desires. Whatever we have desired, from all four directions we have attracted it. We have become whatever our seed desired; we have got what we wished for.

Then there is the man who lives in anger, in turmoil, in greed, in fear, in lust, and asks where the divine is: "The divine? I cannot see it anywhere." When the first cosmonaut returned to the earth, Khrushchev declared in a speech: "Our cosmonaut flew into outer space, but he did not see any God there." It is difficult to refute

Khrushchev. Those who think that God can be found on some moon, on some planet or star, let them understand clearly: if not today, then tomorrow, if not Khrushchev, but someone else will definitely declare that he has checked all the planets and moons and stars and has not found God anywhere. There *have* been people who have attained to the ultimate on this very earth. And there are those who could not attain it even by traveling to the moon and stars.

Wherever the jasmine may grow, on the moon or on the earth, it cannot become a rose. It will only be able to become what its destiny is; it will become what it can be. We may travel to any corner of the world, but we will remain as we are. Wherever we are, we will be able to see, to draw toward us or experience, only that which we ourselves are capable of attracting.

Eyes draw light. If someone were to play the sitar in front of your eyes, the eyes will not be able to hear the sitar playing. And no matter how many lamps you light in front of your ears, those ears will not be able to see the light and know that lamps have been lit. The ears will keep saying: "Where is the light? I cannot hear it anywhere." Now, can light be heard? The eyes will say: "Where is the sitar playing? I cannot see any music. Where is the music?" But music cannot be seen. Whichever sense organ we use to see and understand life, that is how we experience it. For us, the world itself then becomes what we are.

As I explained yesterday we have seven centers. The lowest and the highest centers – the first and the seventh – are the energy storehouses. They do not do anything; they are merely receptacles. They store energy; all the energy is gathered in these centers. The second center, the sex center, is where energy is thrown out, expelled. It is the exit from where the energy flows out. That is why the person who lives in this center becomes increasingly listless, powerless. Gradually all his energy flows out and he is left without vigor.

The sixth center – the one on the forehead exactly between the eyes, which I have called the third-eye chakra – is the exact opposite of the sex center. It is the entrance through which all energy enters your being. From the sex center, energy is thrown out and through the third-eye chakra, energy enters. Hence the more a man lives his life in lust and passion, the lower is his resolve because he is then furthest from his third-eye chakra. The man who lives his life closer to his third-eye chakra, whose attention is focused there, will not even know when lust gradually fades from his consciousness and eventually disappears. This is because the third-eye chakra is the host for all energy, power. It invites it in, takes nourishment from it, drinks from it. The greater the energy that is taken in at the third-eye chakra, the stronger, more powerful, more energetic, more vigorous, and resolute the person becomes.

Between these two centers – the sex center for the expulsion of energy and the third-eye chakra for attracting energy in – there are three other centers: the navel, the heart, and the throat. These are responsible for the internal functioning of the body, they keep it going. Understanding these seven centers rightly is essential for the meditator.

People say we cannot see the divine, we cannot see the soul. But as soon as the center which joins us to the infinite – the seventh center – is activated, the world begins to disappear and the infinite begins to appear. It's not that the world is no more; the world still is, but not as we know it. It becomes the world of the infinite.

Rabiya was a Sufi dervish. In her holy scriptures she read that the Devil was to be hated. In her own book, she crossed through that line.

A friend who was also a dervish was a guest in her home. In the morning he opened the scriptures and saw that the words had been tampered with. He asked Rabiya: "Have you gone mad? Did you change the words? How can scriptures ever be changed?"

Rabiya answered: "I had no choice, I had to amend the text. Since the time I have been able to see the infinite, I cannot see the Devil at all. In the scriptures it says to hate the Devil but I cannot see any Devil. Now wherever I look I see only God. Even if the Devil were to stand in front of me, I would see only God. That the first problem.

"And the other difficulty is that ever since I came to know, there is no hate in me, there is only love. Now how can I hate? Firstly, I cannot see the Devil and secondly I have no hate left in me. That is why I crossed through that line. It is no longer relevant for me."

The day the seventh center becomes active, the experience of everything that was so far unseen, everything that so far could not be known, happens. But why does this happen?

When a child is born, he has no consciousness of any feeling of lust because that center is not yet active. As soon as that center is energized, the world will suddenly seem to change; it will take on a different and new appearance. Once the center within is energized, the world outside begins to change. But the world as it was yesterday is the same today, so what has happened? The world hasn't changed, but the dormant center within has now awakened.

Exactly in the same manner, when the seventh center becomes energized the world remains exactly the same, but now in it something new can be seen. We absorb within ourselves only that which we are capable of absorbing. Everything is available. What Buddha absorbed from the world is still present. Even today, there is absolutely no difficulty in becoming a Buddha. Even today, there is no problem in becoming a Mahavira, neither is there any obstacle to becoming a Rama or a Krishna. All that they attained is still available. We just need to awaken the center within us that can absorb all this.

But we ask the opposite. We ask: "Where is the divine?" We do not ask: "Where is the center that needs to be awakened to experience the divine?" We miss experiencing it because this center remains dormant. All around us there are endless experiences, endless knowledge, endless thoughts. Those thoughts surround us twenty-four hours a day. Whichever thought we encompass in ourselves, whichever center we awaken, thoughts in harmony with that center rush toward us, catch hold of us, engulf us. This needs to be understood.

If one day, in the morning, you lose your temper, you will be surprised that during the whole day numerous instances arise that make you angry. Why on this particular day? You think that from the very morning it has been a bad day; your luck has deserted you. It has nothing to do with luck. From all around, the center that was awakened in the morning has been attracting incidents that are aligned to it – and this continues throughout the day. That is why those who know say that even when going to sleep, sleep with great awareness, for even when you are sleeping, during the night thoughts are being continuously drawn into your consciousness.

All night you dream. These dreams are made up of thoughts that you are drawing to yourself. The man sleeping next to you may be dreaming that he is a sage, you may be dreaming that you are a thief. Do not think that although you are sleeping next to each other you are dreaming the same thing. What significance does a dream have? Whether you dream that you are a sage or you dream that you are a thief, you are only dreaming about that which your mind is awakened to. A sage or a thief: these are only thoughts drawn to you from all sides. The person who sleeps with awareness will attract thoughts of awareness and tranquility from all directions toward himself.

It is also necessary to get up with awareness, so that you journey throughout the day with those thoughts with which you started the day. But more often than not people begin the day in a wrong manner and they end it wrongly. These two periods need great attention. The moments before you sleep should be filled with great awareness, calm, silence, bliss, and prayer. Then in those six to eight hours of sleep you will draw to yourself thoughts of a new world to yourself, a new light, and new ideas. When you get up, the first few moments should be meditative, so that your journey during the full twenty-four hours of that day attracts all that is good, all that is beautiful, all that is true. Whoever is able to manage these two moments will be able to manage all twenty-four hours.

That is why the meditation that I am talking to you about should be done at night before sleeping, and again when you wake up. Both the process of waking and the process of sleeping should begin with meditation. If you can manage these two transition stages rightly, you will find a peacefulness and transformation taking place within yourself.

Keep in mind what I have said: there is a sea of thoughts all around us. Before the radio was invented, we could not even imagine that what was being said in Moscow could be heard in Mumbai: we just did not know this was possible. Similarly, the people in Moscow were not aware that what was being spoken in Mumbai could be heard in Moscow. But now we know. Just by sitting here we cannot hear what is being said in Moscow or Beijing or New York, but the moment we have a radio it changes. It's not the radio which brings the voice to us but the sound waves passing through here. The radio merely captures them.

Much is present all around us but we only catch hold of that which we understand; the rest escapes us. We can absorb only that which is on our level, on our wavelength, which is in tune with the active chakra. Then we see only that, hear only that; we encompass it.

There is an endless web of thoughts all around. Remember: no word ever dies. Nothing in this world ever dies. What I am saying now will never die; there is no way for it to disappear. Whatever has been said becomes immortal and permanent. For time without end, this sound will keep resonating in the universe, will keep echoing and encircling the universe. Any sound once born will endlessly echo, reverberate, in numberless universes.

Scientists believe that it is entirely possible that one day an instrument may be invented which will be able to capture what Krishna said to Arjuna in Kurukshetra. It is very possible that what Jesus said can be captured, what Mahavira spoke in Bihar can be captured because even today those sounds would be resonating somewhere. Whether or not scientists will be able to invent such a device is a matter for speculation. But those who are able to activate their seventh center, even without the aid of any instruments, can grasp all the noblest ideas that have ever been thought on this earth. The wealth of the finest the world has to offer is within their reach, and the experience of living among these waves is unique.

Nietzsche once said: "There was a moment when I felt that I am living a thousand miles beyond time." A thousand miles beyond time? How is it possible for a person to be thousands of miles beyond time? But anyone who has experienced anything on that level knows that from there it appears as if the whole world is in a deep ditch, a ravine, lost in some dark valley, and he is living on the peak of Mount Everest. The experience of standing on such a peak, living on such a peak, happens only after activating our highest chakra. How can this be done?

It is possible to activate it; without activating this chakra in your life you will not be able to enter the temple of the infinite. This chakra can be awakened only with resolve, and this means energizing the third-eye chakra. The resolve then goes deeper and deeper and deeper until it finally activates the seventh and last chakra.

The deeper we can take the meditation technique I have explained – to the maximum depth possible – the more successful we will be in activating this last chakra.

Keep in mind that this chakra does not get energized on its own, it happens only through our effort. Yes, maybe someday it will happen by itself. Perhaps after millions of years, in the course of evolution, it may become activated by itself. But then we would have to wait until that time.

Meditation has one meaning: whatever development nature can bring about in millions of years, the meditator can achieve swiftly, very quickly, in a much shorter time. It is of course possible that after many, many eons, every being will be born in the state that Buddha and Mahavira achieved. But the way of nature is very long, very slow, and very leisurely. The person who wants to speed it up will need to become active; he will need to do something himself. But we do not do anything ourselves. We are a little like something floating in a river, going wherever the current takes us, not even protesting. But if we understand correctly, our not doing anything – just drifting, living life lazily as a part of nature's plan – is the source of the feeling that life is futile. If we want to break out of this sense of worthlessness, something will need to be done.

But what? Praying in temples? Falling at the feet of gurus? Putting vermillion dots on our foreheads? Performing ritual offerings and throwing herbal preparations into the fire? These are ways we have found to escape from having to do the right thing. This is not what we have to do. Doing all these things will achieve nothing. It will only help us deceive ourselves that we are making an effort. Perhaps even the earlier state, where we were merely drifting, was better than this. At least there was no question of us deluding ourselves that we were doing something. At least we were clear in our minds that we were not doing anything, but there was always the possibility that we might do something someday.

When people do such things as counting prayer beads or praying in temples, they begin to believe that they are making an effort and because of this misconception, the possibility of someday making a real effort is lost; it dies unborn. That is why there is no greater harm done to the world than by the various rituals practiced in the name of religion. And there is no greater harm done to mankind than that done by the agents who endorse and promote such religious rituals. The men at whose feet people fall and pray have their hands firmly around the necks of those worshipping people. They are the ones squeezing the life out of the people. But none of this can be seen.

Instead of people doing practices to develop resolve, they have been handed a set of worthless rituals, through which neither resolve is developed, nor willpower strengthened. The practice of these rituals neither leads to the awakening of any centers nor does it generate any vigor in life.

Thousands and thousands of such practices are common in this world. In the name of religiousness, a substitute type of religion, a pseudo religion, a false religion, has spread throughout the world. This false religion has become a huge obstacle and is preventing man from becoming spiritual because he feels that by going to the temple he has done all that needs to be done.

There *is* a temple to which one has to go – the temple within. But the crafty, cunning, and clever man has made another temple, the temple outside, to which he can go, return home and then declare that he has been to the temple. He does not know where the temple is. He does not even realize that someone who goes to the temple never returns; he begins living there. It is the point of no return; nobody comes back from there.

We go to this temple that is outside in the morning and come back. But *how* did we go in there? We are the same as when we left home. A man enters the temple and the same man comes out. Where have we entered a temple? Going inside a temple means that we have reached a place where we are no longer who we were. Only then have we entered a temple, otherwise not.

What does going to a temple mean? A man leaves his house, goes to house *A* or house *B* and returns – does it mean he has come from the temple? Man is extremely wily, very clever when it comes to deceiving himself.

The meaning of going to a temple is inner conversion. Going to a temple implies entering a state of consciousness where we are transformed, where we are no longer who we were before entering. Remember: when we return from that temple it is no longer possible to be who we were earlier. But nobody returns from that temple; if he does, the temple comes with him. Then he begins living in the temple itself. But we do not know where the temple is. We have made it outside; the structure of the temple has been built outside. We go there, offer our prayers to the structure, and return. No, the temple is not outside. The temple is the seventh chakra I have been talking about. Entering this seventh chakra is entering the temple.

People who have known have spoken about the temple inside. We have listened, but we have built the temple on the outside. You enter a temple... On the outside there are walls, inside is the sanctum sanctorum where the image of the deity is placed. All around the sanctum sanctorum there is a walkway, and we walk around the deity seven times. Have you ever thought about why you have to do seven rounds? Have you ever thought about what are you circling? And why is there an image of the deity placed at the center of the circle we are walking around? Why is it called the sanctum sanctorum? What is this round structure? Why is the dome round? What is all this about?

After listening to the people who have spoken about the temple inside, we have built the outside temple in exactly in the same fashion. The dome that you see at the top of the temple is symbolic of the top of man's head. Somewhere in the head, inside a circle, the divine resides – this is how those who have known may have spoken. Only after one has gone around the circumference, completed the journey on the perimeter, is the experience of the one who resides inside possible. This is what they might have said.

But we have built a structure on the outside. We go round and round it and return home. All the sages and saints whom we call mahatmas – who are really only half mahatmas – urge us to go to the temple, say that we must go to the temple. For thousands of years, those poor souls have been repeating that it is necessary to go to the temple. I also say that you must go to the temple, but the temple that they are guiding you to is not a temple at all. The temple is somewhere else; it is within you.

I have heard a story...

Some small children lived in a house. When they were still very young, their parents died in a boat accident. Although they were very young, they thought that even if their parents were no more, they should still do what their parents used to do; there must have been a reason for it. They had seen that after dinner their father used to take a small wooden stick from a cabinet and do something with it.

He used to clean his teeth after his meals and kept a small twig for this purpose. The boys did not know this; they were too young to know what he had been doing. Their teeth didn't need any cleaning with twigs, so they had no reason to know about that. But they did know that their father kept this twig in the cabinet and twice a day, every day, went to the cabinet for some reason. They thought there must be some connection between eating and going to the cabinet – and it must have something to do with the wooden stick.

So after their parents died, they too kept a small wooden stick in the cabinet. They did not know any better. Every day, after their meals, they would go to the cabinet with folded hands and bow their heads to the wooden stick. This became a regular practice.

When they grew up and built a new house, they thought it was time to throw away the small wooden twig and make a new stick out of sandalwood – after all they prayed to it every day. So for their new house they made a beautiful sandalwood stick, and instead of the cabinet they built a small beautiful temple and placed the sandalwood stick inside it. Every day, morning and evening, after their meals, they would go with folded hands to the temple and bow. Generations passed. Their children were born and they built even bigger houses, in turn their grandchildren built bigger and bigger houses. The small cabinet was gradually transformed into a large temple. What was once a small twig had become a massive pillar.

Then one day someone asked them: "What is this all about?"

They replied: "This has been happening in our family for generations. It is a religious practice and anyone who does not follow it is not religious. Some of our children have been corrupted. They do not believe in all this and even refuse to fold their hands and bow before it."

Now the children who do not fold their hands and bow are corrupted, those who do so are very pious. Something like this has happened, is happening. The final truths of life can only be spoken of in terms of symbols. But we hold on to the symbols, tie ourselves down to them – and then we begin worshipping the symbols, forgetting that the symbols just indicate toward something else. The symbols are not the truth, they are merely pointers, guides, to the truth.

As I have said, the seventh chakra is the temple that has to be entered. And the door through which we enter is the third-eye chakra. How can we work on this third-eye chakra? How can we make this chakra come alive, become active, and reach a point where its flowering is complete?

Three small but basic points must be understood. Firstly, the greater the resolve you develop in your life, the more this door will open. But what does resolve mean? Resolve means that whatever you may wish to do is done with all your power, all your capacity. You cannot be split inside, half your mind telling you to do it and the other half urging you not to do it. If the mind is split, disintegrated, fragmented, then the different pieces will clash with each other and all resolve will be destroyed.

Our minds are always divided into different parts, so

much so that even for the minutest of things the mind is split; it is beyond comprehension. There is neither a straight no within us, nor a straight yes; both are present simultaneously. We neither want to go to the left nor to the right; we want to go in both directions at the same time. Then, gradually, the entire resolve fades away.

Our minds are as if we have put bullocks on all four sides of a bullock cart. They pull the cart in all directions. Obviously, the cart does not move, but its parts are pulled apart and weakened. Such chaos is created that even the bullocks get tired and wonder what is happening.

If you examine your own life carefully, you will find that there are bullocks tied to all sides of your cart. There is no single resolve inside; there are twenty-five different resolves. You may not even have realized that totally contradictory resolves are present within you. The person you love is also the person you hate. This will seem surprising, but it may not have occurred to you that any moment your friend can turn into your enemy. There was so much love, then how, within a moment, did it turn into so much hatred?

Hidden right under the love, hatred was waiting for the moment when love moved away so that it could take its place. That is why there is never as much danger from enemies as there is from friends. If an enemy is transformed, he can only change into a friend; the friend is hidden within him. But if a friend is transformed, there is only one possibility for him: he turns into an enemy, for the enemy is hidden within him. That is why for an enemy there is still hope, but not for a friend.

The person you hold in reverence is the same for whom your mind is filled with disdain, just waiting for the right opportunity to appear. For disdain to show its face, the reverence just needs to be thrown aside. Be very wary of people who show a lot of respect, as inside they will be preparing for contempt.

Our mind is in a state of internal turmoil. We are one person on the outside, somebody else on the inside, and whoever we may be, simultaneously we are somebody else too. When you hold someone's hand and say that you love them very much, take a look inside yourself and see what your mind is really saying in that moment. The mind will be asking: "What lies are you uttering; why are you saying such things?"

There was a mystic called Nasruddin. He was in love with the wife of the king of his village. One night he was taking leave of the king's wife. As he was leaving he said to her: "There is no woman as beautiful as you. And the amount I love you – ah, I have neither loved anyone as much before nor can I ever in the future. You are unique."

She was very pleased, very happy, just as when any man says this to a woman. She asked: "Really?"

Seeing her so happy, Nasruddin – he was a very honest man – said: "Wait! Let me also tell you what is going on in my mind. When I said that there is nobody as beautiful as you, inside my mind said: 'Why are you saying this to such an ordinary woman; there are many like her.' I told you that I love you very much, that I have not loved anyone as much as I have loved you. And my mind was laughing inside, saying: 'You have said this to other women too – exactly those words.'"

Man's mind is filled with inner contradictions, all the time overflowing with internal conflicts. If there is internal conflict, resolve can never arise because resolve means one mind. Resolve means a unified mind, integration; resolve means one voice; resolve means one sound. Twenty-four hours a day we are filled with conflicting voices. We need understanding to be able to silence these conflicting sounds. When we say that our faith is firm, that is when we have doubt within. It is strange: whatever we say, exactly the opposite is present within us. This exact opposite within us negates and divides whatever we say. Then our entire personality gets tied up in these conflicts and disappears.

Is it possible to gradually reduce these inner conflicts? – it is possible. First, we will need to be aware so that we do not nurture these conflicts. What I am saying, what I go on saying is: do not revere anyone, then there is no need for irreverence. Do not have faith, then doubt will not arise. Do not be a friend, then there will be no need to become an enemy. Do not be a disciple, otherwise the race to become a guru will begin. It is inevitable, it is already happening and will continue to do so.

Try to avoid the contradiction that is there, try to escape from both aspects so that a state of harmony arises in your consciousness. Do not split yourself by saying that you are a believer, because as soon as you say this half your mind will immediately become a nonbeliever. Find the biggest believer you can and you will also see the nonbeliever within him. The nonbeliever cannot die, it can only be suppressed. Find the biggest nonbeliever and you will also find the believer in him; the believer cannot die. Be neither a believer nor a nonbeliever. Let the contradiction go; do not be split through inner conflicts.

The more a person is able to deeply understand this and escape contradictions, the more he will find a unique sense of calm and balance arising within him. A state of harmony, a unified mind – complete, unbroken, unfrag-mented – begins to arise. This state is what is known as resolve. The more this state is nurtured, the smoother our journey within will be.

But we always see a thing in parts. We say we will be friends or that we will be enemies, nothing is possible in between. We do not realize that it is only "in between" that we can really be. We either say we will have faith, or no faith; either we will have respect or no respect – of the two we choose one option. But someone who chooses one option will keep the other one open. The perspectives will keep changing like the pendulum of a clock swings from one side to the other. But remember: it keeps moving. It swings to one side only so that it can return to the other side. When it is swinging to one side, it has already started moving to the other side. The speed of going to the left, this very momentum, will send it back to the right.

That is why those who know life well laugh when someone says they are their friend and when someone says they are their enemy. Those who understand life laugh when somebody bows to their feet and they laugh when somebody throws shoes at them. This is the pen-dulum of man that keeps swinging without any signifi-cant meaning to it. But what is funny is that even though man is in motion like a pendulum, he is not aware of what he is doing – just moving from one side to the other.

When consciousness is focused, aligned, unified and in harmony, it is in a state of resolve. Whoever is in this state can enter the temple within. If you understand resolve correctly, then it is the key that will open the lock to the chakra I call the *sahasrar* chakra. But we do not have the key to resolve and, unfortunately, we also do not have the key that leads to resolve.

I have heard…

In a very ancient, cultured family a small seven-year-old boy was being sent away to be educated.

His father said to him: "Whoever has gone away from our home to study has never returned before completing his education. It has been a tradition and practice in our family that even when we send a small child there, the child never looks back; we are against anyone looking back. When my father bade me goodbye, sent me away to be educated, he said 'There should be no tears. If tears come to your eyes, then this house will no longer be your home; you will not be able to return. We do not allow people who cry into our house.'

"The same thing I will say to you. Tomorrow at four o'clock in the morning, you will be leaving. A servant will seat you on a horse and then come with you. A mile out from here there is a bend in the road. Up until this point you can see our house, but do not look back. We will be standing on the terrace to make sure that you do not look back because you cannot trust a person who looks back. Do not look back at all."

A small child, just seven years old. He was very nervous. At night his mother reassured him: "Don't worry; it has always been this way." Then she said: "I have heard that once somebody did look back and then this home could no longer be his. Do not look back."

The seven-year-old child could not sleep all night, thinking he would not be able to turn round and see his mother and father, would not be able to see his home, not be able to have tears in his eyes or to look back. Such expectations from a seven-year-old child!

We might say that these people must have been very

heartless, very cruel. If we had been in their place, we would have pampered the boy, given him chocolate. We would have cried, allowed him to cry, shown our love. But this is not love; this is breaking the resolve in the child's personality. Today, everyone in the world thinks this way. Everyone thinks that you must dance around your child, become more of a child than the child. Such children will never be able to develop that determination inside that should be there. Their soul will not develop a spine.

That child left at four o'clock in the cool breeze of the morning. His mother and father did not come to the door to see him off – they must have been very cruel, heartless. The child was seated on a horse. The servant with him said: "Son, do not look back. You are not allowed to look back. You are no longer a little boy; we have great expectations of you. What expectations can you have from a person who looks back? Your father is looking at you from the terrace. How happy he will be if his son doesn't look back all the way up to the bend in the road."

Just imagine what condition the boy would have been in. How much he would have wanted to turn back and take a look. A small, delicate seven-year-old boy! But without turning back, without looking, he turned the corner. Later, the boy wrote that when a mile had passed and he had not turned around, he felt a strange wave of happiness come over him.

He reached the school early in the morning. One of the monks at the school, the one who would be teaching him, met him at the door and said that not everyone could be admitted; there were rules for entry. "Sit down at the door with your eyes closed. You are not to get up or even open your eyes until I return and call you myself. If, in the meantime, you open your eyes, enter, or look around you, then you will be put on your horse and sent back home. Your servant is waiting outside. Remember: no child from your family has ever been sent back. This is the test for your admittance."

The young boy was made to sit by the door. Nobody said to him: "Son, your mother must be sad. Let us make some arrangements for you." Nobody asked him anything. His bags were by his side, his horse tied up outside, the servant waiting. That child, a mere seven-year-old, was made to sit by the door with his eyes closed. Those teachers must also have been very cruel and heartless. But those who know, know that there is no one kinder and more compassionate than those parents and teachers.

The child continued sitting. Other children were now entering the school, somebody pushed him, somebody threw pebbles at him, somebody teased him – children will be children. But he had to keep his eyes closed, come what might, because if he did not keep his eyes closed, he would have to return home. How could he face his father if he was sent back? Nobody in his family had ever come home that way.

The morning sun began to rise, flies were buzzing around him, children were throwing pebbles at him, whoever passed by pushed him. That small child: his eyes closed, his hunger increasing, feeling thirsty. But he could neither open his eyes nor could he get up.

Afternoon came, the sun was directly over his head. What was happening? Nobody came, nobody spoke to him. He continued to sit with his eyes closed. He did not open his eyes, did not blink even once.

It was evening, the sun about to set. He was now

tortured by pangs of hunger. Then the monk, along with ten or fifteen other monks, came, lifted him up, and said: "You have passed the entrance test. You have resolve. Now something can be done. You can enter."

When the child grew up and became a young man he wrote: "Today, when I look back, I realize that those who seemed so heartless at that time were actually filled with compassion."

Our compassion is very strange. It distorts everything, makes everything impotent. When we deal with others, or even with ourselves, we are equally relaxed and lenient. Resolve cannot be developed like this. Developing resolve means something has to be done – something has to be put at stake, some decisions need to be taken – without the need to pause, the need to stop somewhere. It is only under such pressure that resolve can arise.

Here I ask you to meditate. Even fifteen minutes becomes so difficult that I have to call an end to it after ten minutes. Do not imagine that you have been sitting in meditation for fifteen minutes. Seeing your condition, after a mere ten minutes the meditation has to be brought to a close. In fifteen minutes, how many times did you open your eyes? Are you even aware of that? Can resolve ever be born like this? Even for fifteen minutes you cannot sit silently with your eyes closed. Can there be a state more pathetic, more impotent, than this?

Sitting with eyes closed for fifteen minutes has become so difficult. You feel like looking at your neighbor to see what is happening to him. What is happening behind you? Somebody is breathing very fast – what is happening to him? You are bothered about what is happening to everyone around but not at all concerned that you are not able to sit with your eyes closed, even for fifteen minutes. You are not concerned about what is happening to you, not worried at all about this, not worried that you no longer have any resolve.

When a volcano erupted in Pompeii, the whole city was aflame. A soldier was on night duty at a crossroads. His shift changed only at six in the morning when another soldier would come and stand at his place.

The volcano erupted at two o'clock at night. The whole city of Pompeii was in chaos and all the inhabitants were trembling. Fire was everywhere, the whole city up in flames, everyone was running.

As they ran, the people asked the soldier: "Why are you standing there?"

The soldier replied: "My shift changes at six in the morning. How can I move away before that?"

The people said: "Are you mad? At this time, there is no question of duty, you will die! Six in the morning will not come; the whole city is in flames."

The soldier replied: "That may be so. But this is the opportunity, I will know then whether I am a soldier or not. How can I move before six o'clock? If I survive till six in the morning, then I will leave my post. Otherwise it's up to God; then I cannot be blamed."

It is said that the soldier died there, burned at his post! Everyone from the city of Pompeii escaped. But there is no statue in memory of those people. Only a statue of the soldier stands on that spot. There was only one man who deserved to be called a man in that city. He had an inner strength; he had a mind that could withstand anything.

But what about us? Forget Pompeii, even if someone lights a cigarette nearby we open our eyes. If somebody coughs next to us we open our eyes. What kind of a character is this? Which temple can we enter with this kind of personality? Like this, you will not be able to enter any temple. Nothing is stopping us except we ourselves. Just a little resolve, a little strength, a little courage, a little effort is needed. Then it is possible.

Every day people come to me and say that they have meditated for a day but nothing has happened yet. People are very strange, bizarre; they say such extraordinary things. After meditating for just one day, they think they have done God a great favor and it should be written in his ledger that he is now indebted to them. Nothing has happened as yet, nothing has been seen, a meeting with the infinite has not happened. Nothing has happened even though they sat with eyes closed for fifteen minutes – during which time they must have opened their eyes fifteen times! In our persona there is nothing that can be termed the call, the inner voice; it is just not there. Until it is there, there can be no progress on the path of dharma. That is why I say that resolve is the first basic key.

The second thing is: what is resolve? It is not necessary to understand what is meant by resolve; it is essential to do small experiments with resolve. The more you practice, the more it will develop, otherwise it never will. You will need to start from today, from now; if you wait until tomorrow, then too it will never develop. So the second key is: whether you have resolve or not, begin experimenting in that direction. It will grow slowly, but it will certainly grow.

A man stands by the riverside and says: "I want to learn swimming." The coach says: "Come, step in the water"

The man replies: "Until I learn swimming, I will not step in the water. Why should I invite danger? Once I learn swimming, I am ready to go in the water, but not until then."

Now it is very difficult to teach him swimming. In order to teach him, he will have to go in the water, and the first time he will need to do it without knowing how to swim. His skill at swimming can only develop if he steps in the water. Swimming is not something that falls from the sky into someone's lap. That skill can be learned only by swimming. It is the end result of splashing around, and can only happen when we begin by moving our arms and legs in the water.

People say they want meditation, they want ultimate peace. How will you get this? Is it kept somewhere so that you can go and pick it up? No, it is not kept anywhere; it is the creation of your complete and total effort. It is your own creation; if you try, you will get it. If you move your arms and legs a little today, there will be some progress tomorrow, a little more the day after, and the time will come when you realize that the splashing around has been transformed into swimming.

What is swimming? It is that very splashing and moving around of arms and legs, but with a little more skill, a little more organized. When you throw a man in the water on the first day, then too he only splashes around. The difference to swimming is that the movement of the arms and legs is disorganized, but with daily practice it becomes organized.

When you sit in meditation today, the resolve will be disorganized. Tomorrow, it will be a little better. The day after tomorrow a little more progress will have taken place. And what is the hurry? Why the rush that it must happen today? For minor and worthless things in life we are able to wait for years.

The first point: Resolve.

The second point: Resolve will come not with understanding but with effort, by doing.

And the third point: for development of resolve, patience is the biggest virtue. It will not happen merely because you want it to. Great patience and serenity is required. The more patience you have, the sooner it will happen. The more impatient you are, the more difficult it will become. Impatience shows that resolve is not being developed. Impatience shows that resolve will never be developed, because in the soil of impatience nothing can be created.

I have heard...

In Korea, two monks, one old and the other young, carrying a lot of books with them, had just crossed a river in a boat. It was evening and the sun was about to set. The village was far away and the path led through dense jungle and mountains. They were in a hurry to reach the village.

They told the boatman: "We want to reach the village before the sun sets because we have heard that the entrance to the village is closed at sundown. At night it will be dangerous to travel the path through the forest. Will we be able to reach?"

Tying up his boat, slowly, without any hurry, the boatman said: "Certainly you will reach, but go slowly. If you hurry, then I cannot say whether or not you will reach."

The monks said to each other: "Have we asked a madman this question? He is advising us to go slowly and then we will reach, but if we go fast, he is not sure whether we will reach!"

As the sun was about to set, they started running. Even then the boatman said: "Friends, do not hurry. I have never seen a man in a hurry reach that village." Hearing this, they started running even faster.

This is the peculiarity of man; his mind is like this. They still thought the man was crazy, asking them to walk slowly.

They ran. A little further along the path, with the sun setting, darkness growing, the old monk fell over a rock and seriously injured his knees. The pages of the books scattered, blowing in the wind. The young monk was running here and there trying to retrieve the pages.

Just then the boatman strolled by, humming softly, swinging his stick. He said: "See, what I had anticipated, happened. Why this impatience? I told you to go slowly on this mountain road. You can only reach the village if you are not impatient. Often this happens, frequently it happens, that people come to me and say they want to reach the village quickly. I tell them to go slowly, but they do not listen – and they fall."

The old monk replied: "At the time, this thought did not occur to us."

You will have to wait for a long time; tremendous patience is needed for the journey within. You have to be prepared to wait for infinity, for this is the search for the divine. This is not something worth two paise that you run to the market and buy. It is not possible to just run and get it. It *is* available, it can be attained; in fact it can be attained right now and right here. But the one who desires to achieve it today and right now, will not even be able to move toward it. With great patience...

But what does patience mean? Patience does not mean any lessening of effort; patience does not mean lowering of energy. Energy has to be total, effort has to be intense, but patience has to be infinite. Be prepared for the journey: if not today then tomorrow, if not tomorrow then the day after, or the day after that – we will wait.

Little children sometimes sow mango seeds. A short while later they dig them up to see if they have sprouted or not. They are very impatient, waiting for the hours to pass. Then after an hour or so they again dig them up to see if anything has happened. Nothing has, so they are greatly disappointed. For a seed to sprout it is necessary for it to remain underground. It has to remain silent in the darkness, so that it can break its own shell and sprout.

Our state is like that of the little children. For two or three minutes we say "Who am I? Who am I?" and then we think "Oh, nothing has happened yet." You have dug the seed out. You look around and see that the others are still meditating, haven't gone anywhere. Again you say it for two or three minutes, but then again the thought comes that nothing is happening, it is taking too long. This way it will not happen, it cannot happen.

So remember these three points: you need resolve, for resolve you need to make an effort, and when you make an effort you need patience. If these three things are complete, then there is no reason for the goal to remain distant. The goal is always very near. If the traveler is skillful, he can reach now, but if the traveler is not skillful, then for life after life he can stray and never reach his goal.

These are some of the things I wanted to tell you.

Now we will sit for our experiment. Keep these things in mind. Friends who are standing should realize that their responsibility is greater than that of those who are sitting down. Compared to yesterday, a few more friends are here today. A few more is not a large number. Some friends are sitting very close to each other, talking. This is rather impolite, incorrect. Those who do not want to do the experiment need not do it, but they should not make the mistake of disturbing those who wish to do it. Perhaps there are some new friends here today, so I will briefly explain the process to them.

For participating in this experiment, first you have to sit with your spine straight. Second, all five fingers of one hand should be intertwined with the fingers of the other hand. The clasped hands should be in your lap. As the intensity increases inside, the fingers will clasp more tightly, start trembling. The spine has to be straight, eyes closed, lips together, and in your head, with great intensity, great resolve, with one voice, with one tone, you have to ask "Who am I?"

What is the point of asking this? As the fervor and intensity of the question increases, this question – "Who am I?" – begins to penetrate and go deep within. We ourselves do not know who we are, but the ultimate core of life within us will definitely know who we are. The day our question reaches this inner core, we will immediately get the answer to that question. But, meanwhile, do not answer the question yourself.

You ask "Who am I?" and the answer comes "I am Brahma." A boy sitting here yesterday was saying the opposite and he was right. He was saying "I am a ghost." That was more correct. Man being Brahma is doubtful, but being a ghost is definite! You do not have to give any reply – whether you are Brahma or a ghost; do not reply at all. You just have to ask "Who am I?"

This inquiry, this question, has to go as deep as possible within. The greater the intensity of the question, the deeper the question will go. The deeper it goes – the greater the intensity, the greater the resolve – the greater will be the experience of a wonderful peace and calm in your mind. As the mind gathers all its energy, it becomes peaceful. The total mind has to be concentrated on this question. It is very simple, but it is simple only if you do it. If you do not do it, nothing is simple.

Chapter 4

Peace: The Shadow of Truth

My beloved ones.
A friend has asked:

Osho,
Are you a socialist? A communist?

The question is very interesting. If existence is a communist, then I too am a communist. Existence must be a communist, for from its viewpoint nobody is unequal, everyone is equal. When someone sees everyone as equal, then even if others see some dissimilarity, he would want them to gradually all become equal. Mahavira must have been a communist; also Buddha and Jesus. Although no one ever asked them this. And Gandhi must surely have been a communist. In fact, someone *did* ask Gandhi this question and he replied: "I am more of a communist than any communist." If considering the welfare of everyone, wishing for the progress of all, desiring the good of all, is communism, then how can any spiritual man be anything but a communist?

But in another sense I am not a communist at all.

The truth is that I do not believe in any "isms," any creed, any doctrine. Communism too is an "ism," a doctrine, a belief, a creed, a sect. It is one of the newest religions in the world. It too has its own priests, its own temples; it has its Mecca, its Kashi, and its Kaaba. The Kremlin is for the communist what Mecca is for the Muslim, Kashi for the Hindu. The book *Das Kapital* by Karl Marx is to the communist what the Gita, the Bible, and the Koran are to their followers. In that sense, I am not a communist. I do not believe in any doctrine.

I am neither a communist, a socialist, a fascist, nor a Gandhian – nor do I wish that anyone should fragment himself in that way. Whenever a person gets tied to a doctrine it is a sign of slavery; he becomes enslaved. Anyone who is chained to a sect loses the freedom of his consciousness. From the very moment anyone thinks that a creed is his belief he begins to lose touch with the truth. Either you can have truth or you can have belief; either you can be spiritual or belong to a sect. And all sects, whether religious or political, only work toward enslaving man's consciousness.

So I am not involved with any sect. If I used such words, I would more correctly say that I am an anti-sectarian, an anarchist – although *anarchist* is certainly not the right word. An anti-sectarian cannot belong to any sect because *anti-sectarian* means one who is not part of any sect. But my words often create a lot of confusion. The doubts that arise from my words are such.

I am reminded of a story from Buddha's life which I will tell you in order to explain.

One morning Buddha and the monk Ananda were passing through a village. On the way, they met a man who said: "I am a believer, I believe in God. Do you also believe in God?"

Buddha replied: "God? God does not exist. Where is the question of believing in him?"

The man was taken aback. He thought to himself: "Buddha seems to be an atheist."

Ananda was also very surprised that Buddha had replied so abruptly that there was no God so there was no question of believing in him. But he kept quiet.

In the afternoon, another man came from the village and said to Buddha: "I am an atheist, and do not believe in God. What do you think – is there a God?"

Buddha replied: "Only God is, nothing else."

That man thought to himself: "This Buddha seems to be a believer."

After hearing both answers, Ananda was in great difficulty. The first man had gone away satisfied that Buddha was an atheist and the second man that Buddha was a believer. But what should Ananda understand? Still he kept quiet, thinking he would ask Buddha that night when they were by themselves.

In the evening another incident happened. A third man came and asked: "I do not know whether there is a God or not – what do you think?"

Buddha kept quiet and did not answer.

That night Ananda said: "I am very restless, not able to sleep at all. What is all this? In the morning you said one thing, in the afternoon another, and in the evening nothing at all. These three responses are very contra-dictory."

Buddha said: "But I did not say anything to you, so why were you listening? My answers were for those other people."

Ananda said: "I had no choice as I was with you and heard all three answers. Those three men went away happy, but now I have a big problem. Just what *are* you?"

Buddha replied: "I just am."

"But why did you give three different answers?" asked Ananda.

Buddha said: "If you want to understand, you can understand. The man who comes to me and asks 'God is not. What do you think?' wants my endorsement for his nonbelieving, so that he can go away satisfied. What he believes then becomes even stronger. I want to break every belief, so I told him 'God? God is.' I want to shatter his conviction, because anyone who just believes is a slave. He will never be able to find the truth, irrespective of what his belief is.

"The man who came and asked 'God is, do you believe this?' also wants my validation for his belief. When I replied that God is definitely not, so there is no question of believing, I wanted to shake his belief too, so that he becomes free and can begin to seek the truth.

"The third man who came had no belief. He did not know whether God is or not. I thought that it was good that he did not know. That is why I kept quiet, was silent, so that he may come to know."

Right up until today it has not been possible to decide whether Buddha was a believer or a nonbeliever – academics still debate about this. They will never be able to decide because Buddha was neither a believer nor a nonbeliever. Buddha had no views on this. He wanted everyone to be free of belief, because whoever is free of it can reach the truth.

This kind of a problem happens with me from morning to evening. You hear me speak against one thing and then are troubled thinking "Surely this man must be the opposite of this." If I have spoken against capitalism, then I must be a communist. But I am against capitalism as well as communism.

I am against any "ism." My desire is for a society which is not governed by any "ism." I am against all "isms," against all sects. I do not belong to any sect. That is why I am faced with another problem: all those who belong to a sect consider me to be their enemy – and there is no man who does not belong to one sect or another. That is the reason people find it difficult to consider me their friend.

No, I am neither a communist nor anything else. I keep my eyes open, observe, and then say whatever seems right to me. That right could be anyone's. What seems wrong to me, I say is wrong. That wrong could be anyone's. I would like you also to not get caught up in any sect, any "ism."

It is possible to make a sect around me too; camps and cults can be built around me. Some friends are starting to have the misconception that they are my followers. I do not have any followers, neither do I want any followers because that makes it another sect and means you get tied to me. I want man to be free of everything. He has always been tied to something, tied to something or other. I am not concerned with the name of the peg he is tied to. My concern is *why* he is tied to it. It is not right for a man to be fastened to a peg, whether that peg be Gandhi or Marx, or even me. I want a man to be free of all pegs. Whatever peg or stake I speak against, followers of it begin to think that I must then be endorsing the opposite – some other stake to tie people to!

I am not trying to tie you to anything. I want the mind to be free. The mind that remains free of everything attains to the ultimate reality. That is the only requirement: an unclinging mind, a consciousness that is free.

I am not part of any sect. I have never been part of any sect nor could I ever be. I am against the very concept of sects. I am not against any particular sect, just against the concept. Wherever it exists I get the offensive smell of slavery. Whatever the name – Gandhiism, Communism, Hinduism, Jainism, Mohammedanism – it makes no difference. Understand what I am saying: whenever the mind gets attached to any "ism," its journey toward the divine stops. It is as if you are trapped under a rock, you cannot get up, your wings have been clipped. If you want your consciousness to have wings, then never get tied to anyone or anything.

When I say something against any celebrated or eminent person, you become agitated; you think I am against these people. If you think I am against eminent people, then it will be very difficult to find people who love them! I am not against eminent people. I am not even against Godse, who murdered Gandhi, so how can I be against Gandhi himself? When I speak against an eminent person, then I am not speaking against the person but against his doctrine, against the stake that you are tied to. I am trying to shake it so that you may be free. And you praise that doctrine, that stake, so much that the praise itself becomes the means of binding you. That is why I try to shatter the praise too. Never think that I have any personal enmity toward these people.

But we have little understanding, it's so poor – and for the person who is tied to something, who is prejudiced, the understanding is even poorer. Someone who has a belief cannot have understanding, someone who has a principle to follow cannot have understanding, because they are chained from the very beginning. They begin to see everything from that enslaved position, through the spectacles of a slave. He is incapable of seeing the point. He cannot understand the meaning, the purpose, and where it is pointing.

What I am just pointing out, indicating, is for you to drop everything so that you can turn in. Don't be tied to something outside, so that the flower within can bloom. The one who is tied outside cannot reach within; one who is tied anywhere is still tied. And being bound is an obstacle on the way to finding godliness.

Only those who do not have rocks of principles, dogmas, and creeds weighing down on their chests can fly in that open sky which is infinite, that sky which is the ultimate truth, that sky which is total knowing. Therefore, understand clearly that I am not concerned with any sect. And if a new world is to be created, then it has to be one without any "isms," where there is no pressure to belong to any sect.

I have always believed that a supporter of any sect is incapable of understanding the truths of life. His whole effort is directed toward trying to prove that his doctrines are verified by life's truths. For him, his "ism" is the most important thing; the truths of life are not as important, they are secondary. His beliefs are primary, and life's truths should only prove his doctrines to be correct. But the situation is exactly the opposite: no sect is superior to the prime truths of life. So live according to the truths of life, not to your "isms."

For thousands of years, man has been living according to his beliefs. As the older "isms" become a little stale, new ones take their place. When the old chains become rusty, we make new, shiny chains. Even when we have broken the old chains, we quickly bind ourselves with the new ones, declaring with pride that we are free of the old chains.

If you escape being a Hindu but become a communist, there is no difference. The situation hasn't changed, only the name of the chain. If you escape being a Jaina but become a Gandhian, then you have made a fool of yourself. You've escaped from one sect but got entangled with another; you have not escaped from the trap of sects. The soul has not been able to free itself; it is still trapped. Man does not survive in sects. What survives is the sect, but the man is finished.

I want every person to be free, a flower in full bloom, flowering to its full potential. That is why I am not involved with any sect – not in any way whatsoever. In order for us to create a new and worthwhile world, a free and liberated consciousness is a must.

Another friend has asked:

Osho,
Why do you spare everyone else and speak only against Gandhi?

Because I cannot conceive of a man of greater significance than Gandhi and also because I used to believe that if I speak against Gandhi, then people in this country will be forced to think. But I have been disappointed. There was no thinking, only abuses and slander.

I was very surprised, as I had always thought that the followers of Gandhi were nonviolent – but that was

119

a misconception. I had thought that if I criticize Gandhi, then his followers would ask me to come and meet them, to discuss with them, to explain my viewpoint to them, to talk about what is right and what is wrong. But not one of them did. On the contrary, the few followers who occasionally used to come and listen to me disappeared; they vanished without a trace.

I had not expected that after thirty to forty years of hard work, the thought process that Gandhi had labored hard to establish would disappear in a flash. But our understanding is so limited. Those who are intelligent know that even my criticism of Gandhi was actually furthering his work. But who can explain that to the dull and the foolish!

Gandhi's work and vision died with his death. The fact is that it died even before his demise. Once this happened, Gandhi longed for his own death. In order to revive his work it is necessary that we begin to think again. So I had hoped that a shock would be useful; the country would begin to think anew. Then I realized that there is no point in giving a shock to those who are already dead, no use at all. What I have experienced in the past two to three months has been very revealing, very eye-opening: this country has lost the ability for introspection. We have totally stopped thinking.

It is easy to discuss with a person like me because I never claim that what I am saying is the only truth. To fight with me cannot be easy, as I make it clear that whatever I say could be right or could be wrong. Discussion is possible, conclusions can be made. All I want is that there should be a climate in the country where some introspection, some discussion, some dialogue is possible – that is all I desire. But it does not happen.

If I criticize something, then from the other side a storm of abuse starts. Instead of debating whether what I have said is right or not, my statement is put to one side and a totally different direction is taken. This is extremely unfortunate and very damaging for the future of India – it is difficult to even imagine how harmful. But if not today, surely tomorrow, we will have to consider this matter.

I love Gandhi, there is no question of any enmity. My friends ask me if I am his enemy. I am nobody's enemy; I am incapable of enmity, and because I cannot be an enemy I can speak my mind clearly and openly. At least about our own people we should be able to speak openly and honestly. But somehow we have become so entrapped with fear that even about them we cannot speak openly and candidly.

What I wanted could not happen. A lot of things *did* happen, were written about, talked about, but the thought process that was to be set in motion could not be achieved. India has lost its capacity to think. People thought that perhaps I wanted to throw aside the idol of Gandhi and put myself on a pedestal instead.

I am against all idols, so why would I want to put myself on a pedestal? Is it necessary to remove someone from his position to make room for yourself? There is so much space available in the world that you can go anywhere and make an idol of yourself. Why is there any need to destroy anybody's idol? As there are so many foolish people in the world, even if one of them moves somewhere else, there isn't going to be a shortage of idol worshippers. They will just find others to take his place.

So many gods are worshipped – is there any shortage? There are almost three hundred religions in the world and nobody knows how many gods and goddesses each of them has. In India alone, there are thirty-three million gods and goddesses – nearly one god for each person! Can there be any problem here finding someone to worship your idol?

What is the need to destroy anybody's idol? Destroying idols will only create a lot of problems: if the gods take offence, then it will become very difficult to establish your own idol. What is practical here is to honor and admire all the gods and goddesses, and then quietly make a small place for yourself. Then everything becomes simple.

But I do not wish to make a place for myself, do not want to found any sect or have followers, people worshipping me. All I want is that the country should wake up, should begin to think. People should begin to think, to discuss, to observe and not remain blind. But it seems as if we have taken a vow to remain blind. If someone tries to wake us up, we are angry: "Why are you disturbing our sleep? We are sleeping peacefully, having beautiful dreams, and you are disturbing us."

I am now beginning to feel that by telling someone to think, I'm making him my enemy. That person becomes angry. Not thinking is comfortable, thinking brings discomfort because the moment you start to think, something in life seems to be false and a change happens. If someone thinks about himself, then he will feel the need to change himself. If the thinking is about the outside world, then society will need to change. Thinking is the first step in the revolution process. The moment thinking starts, transformation is inevitable.

Hence if you want to save yourself from the trouble of change then the first necessity is: never think. Remember this basic truth – never think! This brings great comfort.

A man can sleep deeply, and he does not need to struggle in life; he just goes through life half-dead until he finally dies. This has been our destiny for thousands of years. This was our foundation stone – never think.

That is why when anyone forces us to think, it doesn't make us happy, grateful or thankful; it just makes us angry. We are angry that something or someone has pushed us into thinking, although we should really be grateful to him. It's the man who allows us to sleep whom we thank, the person who gives us opium and tells us to take it and sleep without any worry. We are grateful to him for giving us the opium pills. Now we can sleep peacefully.

A friend has asked a question which I had thought of ignoring, but considering the context maybe it would not be appropriate to do so. He has asked:

Osho,
Did you ever have any contact or association with Gandhi?

When he was alive, I had very little contact with him. But since his death, I have been deeply involved with him. When he was alive, I was very young. Only once was there a brief contact, a fleeting meeting, but a meeting of that kind has no meaning. But ever since his death I have had a regular involvement with him. It's not only in thoughts that I mean I am in contact with him, there is an association on a deeper level too. I was thinking of avoiding this question because it might be very difficult to understand my reply. As someone has asked, I will answer, but it is not necessary for you to believe what I say.

We normally think that we can have a relationship only with those who have a physical form. We also believe that we can interact only with those who are present among us. These beliefs are unscientific and fundamentally wrong. Relationships are totally different. Two people can be thousands of miles away and the connection between them can be as strong as between two people sitting next to each other. Now even science has validated this.

In the past, only those people whose work was focused on the mysterious world within the self had this belief, an esoteric belief. They knew that thousands of miles is no distance at all. If a person knows the art of connecting with another internally, then he can do so even when thousands of miles separate them – for thousands of years people used to relate this way. Now, science has validated that this is not merely a possibility, but a fact. This endorsement has come from the most unexpected quarters. The first validation came from Russia: distances of thousands of miles are immaterial and thoughts can be communicated over vast distances through telepathy.

A scientist, Fedyaev, was successful in an experiment to establish a connection over fifteen hundred miles. Sitting in Moscow, he succeeded in sending a mental message to a man sitting in a park in the city of Tbilisi.

In Tbilisi, a thousand miles away from Moscow, a man was sitting on a bench in a park. He was just a stranger, out for a walk, who had sat down on the bench to relax. Let's assume he sat down on a bench numbered eleven.

He was being observed. Fedyaev and his colleagues, speaking on the phone to someone in the park, were told that at such and such a time a man came and sat down on a bench. Fedyaev was asked to send a telepathic message to him saying that he should immediately fall asleep. Fedyaev communicated his thoughts to the man, suggested to him that he should "Go to sleep... Sleep..." One thousand miles away, the man slowly closed his eyes and lay down to sleep.

It could also have been possible that the man was tired, that's why he went to sleep. So the friend in the park said: "Fine, he has gone to sleep; it is now such and such time, please wake him up immediately. Then I can be sure, otherwise it is quite possible that he just fell asleep on his own."

From that long distance, Fedyaev suggested to the man: "Wake up now!" And the stranger opened his eyes and got up.

The friend in the park asked the stranger: "Did you experience anything strange?"

He replied: "I did feel something. When I went to sleep, I felt as if somebody was asking me to go to sleep. But I was tired, so I thought it must be my own mind suggesting this. I went to sleep. But on waking up I also felt as if somebody was asking me to wake up."

Fedyaev did many more experiments after this. The real purpose was to be able to establish telepathic contact – communication through thoughts – with astronauts because in space there is a possibility that the instruments could break down and then no communication at all would be possible. Once the instruments stop functioning, there is no contact possible with the astronaut. It would then be difficult to even ascertain if he was in difficulty or had disappeared into infinite space. If external instruments stop functioning, it is essential that internal instruments take over. They are working toward that. Otherwise space journeys are very risky.

Just as it is possible to establish a connection with people many miles away, there are also ways to establish a link with people who are no longer alive. To us, this appears even more difficult. You will find it strange when you hear that up to five hundred years after Mahavira's death, some of his beloved followers claimed that Mahavira was still in touch with them. That is why it took five hundred years for books on Mahavira to be written. They were written at a time when it was believed there was no longer anybody suitable, or with the ability, to establish an internal connection of the spirit. Afraid that Mahavira's voice would be lost, they transcribed it.

For thousands of years, as long as the possibility of maintaining an interaction existed, a direct relationship, with people who were no longer alive, books were not written – there was no need to write books about them. You will be surprised when you realize that books not only represent man's development, but, in a sense, also his deterioration. For thousands of years, the Vedas were not written. For thousands of years, no significant manuscripts were written. That manuscripts were written at all was a matter of compulsion. For five hundred years after Mahavira's death, no need was felt to write books about him because it was possible to ask Mahavira directly. But when there were no longer people with that ability, it became necessary to write scriptures. The Buddhist scriptures were written one hundred and fifty years after Buddha's death.

Today, I can say, there is not a single person among Mahavira's followers who can establish a connection with him. But among Buddha's followers there are still a few who can connect with him. It is even more miraculous in the case of Jesus: among his followers there are many more who are capable of establishing a connection to him.

A religion in which it is possible to establish a direct link to its source appears to be alive. But the moment the link breaks, that living relationship dies. Throughout his life Gandhi worked hard, but he never bothered about whether or not there was anyone around him with whom he could establish a relationship after his death.

But it is not as if only Mahavira and Buddha did this; it is still being done. Even after the death of Madame Blavatsky, a relationship continued between her and Annie Besant. After her death, Annie Besant continued to maintain a connection with J. Krishnamurthi. But Krishnamurthi separated himself from the theosophists and because there was no one else who could establish a connection with either Madame Blavatsky or Annie Besant, the theosophy movement died.

It is more than possible to maintain links with people who are dead; on the contrary, it is difficult to establish connections with living people because the body always gets in the way. Since you have asked, I will say that I did not have any relationship with Gandhi during his lifetime. But after he was no more, I have tried my best to establish a relationship with him. I would also like to tell you that if you try, you can maintain such links with anyone. It is not that Gandhi has been reborn somewhere. For him, rebirth will be very difficult because so far there is no womb worthy of giving rebirth to a person like him. The wait can be very long.

But this is a different issue and I will not dwell on it because nothing can be said about it; there is nothing to be considered about it, nothing can prove it. Therefore I will leave this issue aside; only because the subject came up did I mention it.

I can tell you that I have not criticized Gandhi without discussing it with him. Otherwise, I would never have done it; I would never have raised the issue. It was only when I was convinced that the criticism was justified, would have the approval of Gandhi, that I do so. But now I feel as if it is not worth bothering about. There does not seem to be any point in working with Gandhi. His followers already consider him to be dead, and to speak about a dead person does not seem right to them. They keep writing to me, asking me why I insist on talking about somebody who is dead. People like Gandhi do not die. But people do not understand this and consider them dead. The reason for this is that there is no one who can establish a relationship with such people.

My entire effort is to prepare some people, so that they can experiment a little with establishing a connection, a relationship, of the kind that I have been talking about. But preparation is a very distant dream; even to come near me a thousand obstacles will be put in their way. Therefore, at a very deep level, the esoteric work that is possible, the fountains of sensitivity that can be unlocked within, remain unreachable and unattained.

The earth becomes poorer by the day, because all means of forming a connection with the wisest of the souls who are still present have been rendered impotent. We must revive these skills. We see only what is on the surface and not what is within. There is no question of us looking within because we do not have any life there.

What I have just said is like going to a blind man and saying "I can see light, I am connected to the sun."

He will respond "What sun? What light? You must be mad! Where is the sun? Where is the light?" The blind man does not realize that he has no eyes. No man is willing to accept that he lacks anything. He will say that there is nothing like a sun, that you are mistaken. That is why there is not much point in talking about sight to a blind man; he will not be able to understand and will be in difficulty.

My problem is that what I want to say to you, I am not able to say, and what I do say appears to be incomplete. Whom should I be speaking to? And the meaning that is extracted from my words is even stranger, and surprising. Then the thought slowly comes to me that those who became silent after knowing must have had a reason for their silence. How long can one hit one's head against a wall?

In India there was a monk, Bodhidharma. He was a unique and strange person. He never faced anybody when he spoke to them. If you ever went to meet him – of course, you probably won't as he will never come to Mumbai and you won't go anywhere to meet him – you would be astonished to see that he has his back toward you and is facing a wall.

Many people asked him: "What kind of behavior is this? We have come to ask you some questions and you sit facing the wall."

Bodhidharma responded: "It is more convenient this way."

The people would persist and ask: "But what is the meaning of this?" Then Bodhidharma would explain.

"When I look at you and speak, it seems as if I am hitting my head against a wall. So when I look at a wall

129

and speak, there is at least one certainty: the wall will definitely not listen and will not misunderstand. Looking at a man while speaking is difficult. There the wall is equally solid, but it is dangerous too, for it misunderstands."

Bodhidharma then said: "When a man comes to me who is not a wall, then certainly I will speak to him face-to-face."

For nine years that man kept facing a wall. He must have been a man of great resolve because turning away from people is not easy, it is very difficult. You feel sorry for them and want to say something to them which could help. There the problem begins: after speaking you realize that what you said was not heard; something else has been heard, something that was never said.

For nine years he kept looking at that wall. In India, for nine years, he did not meet anybody face-to-face; he just kept looking at the wall. From India he went to China where a man came to him and said: "Are you going to turn your face toward me, or shall I cut my head off?"

Immediately Bodhidharma turned toward him and said: "Are you that man?"

The man who is ready to cut his head off can listen. In fact, once you face the truth, there is every possibility, every likelihood, that your old head – your old ego, your old notions, everything you know, your opinions, your scriptures, your this and that – will have to be cut off.

Bodhidharma said: "The man who can cut off his head has come. I will now have to face him to speak to him."

Such people have disappeared. There is hardly anyone who is willing to listen to those who are alive, so what are the chances of people starting a relationship with those who are dead?

The world is not composed of only what you can see and hear. It does not consist of only what you can see with your eyes and hear with your ears. The world goes beyond your eyes and ears; there is a lot more to it. Present all around you, near you, are lots of living beings, souls. But you can neither see them nor feel any connection with them. You do not even know that there is somebody present.

If you ever read about the life of Mahavira, then you will find a very strange incident. Historians are amazed at it and believe that it must be a lie because history records only that which the eyes can see. And those records, too, can be seen by thousands of different people in a thousand different ways. But the story can be believed...

Edmund Burke was writing a book about the history of the world. He had completed half the book. Some fifteen hundred pages had been written. No man had ever attempted to write such an elaborate history of the world before. He had toiled day and night and spent thirty years of his life writing.

One day, as he was writing, he suddenly heard a commotion outside. He saw some of his neighbors running outside his house, so he went outside and asked: "What has happened?"

The neighbors replied: "Someone has been murdered behind your house." Burke ran with them.

The corpse was there, the murderer had been caught, and a large crowd had gathered. One man was asked what had happened. He said one thing. Another man was asked the same question; he said something else. A third man was questioned and he came up with another story. But they were all eye witnesses.

Burke said: "This happened right in front of you. How is it that no two versions agree? It happened behind my house, the corpse is still there – the blood still flowing – the murderer has been caught, a whole crowd is here, but no two people can agree on what has happened. Everyone tells a different story."

Burke went inside and burned the book he was writing, set fire to thirty years' effort. He said: "I am trying to ascertain what happened two thousand years ago, but people with eyes cannot agree on what just occurred behind my house. It is all useless. History is worthless."

He set fire to his work.

He was a wise man. If other historians were also wise, they too would realize the worthlessness of history and set fire to their books.

The incident in Mahavira's life that is often repeated is this: many thousands of people were listening to him and many thousand divine souls were also listening. Now those divine souls could not be seen by anyone, so how could they be listening? Historians would say "We were present, we could see the people, but we could not see any divine souls. How is it possible to see them?"

But it is a fact that there are forms of life more advanced than man and when a person like Mahavira speaks not only humans listen, divine souls listen, too. But this makes sense only for those who can understand. For the blind there is no point in saying such a thing. A lot of things have to be left unsaid, they cannot be spoken about. I wish for a time to come when such things can be discussed. For that it is necessary that people are prepared, so that one day we can talk about such things.

But now, slowly, I am also beginning to feel that I am

making the same mistake that many have made before me – and they failed. This failure is very ancient, goes back a long way. But again and again, I feel like making one more attempt. I know that people crucified Jesus and shot Gandhi. They will continue with their old habits; they will not make an exception in my case. But still the mind says: "Let me make one more attempt, what is the harm?" What will anyway one day disappear, what difference does it make whether it dies on its own, or someone else erases it? What is the difference? That is why I am making one more attempt.

What enmity is there between me and Gandhi? Who can have any animosity toward lovable people like him? Mine is a different kind of effort, and maybe one day you will be able to understand it. I will keep trying, keep hammering on your head, in the hope that one day a realization may come that yes, something of this kind is possible. My aim is just that.

Another friend has asked:

Osho,
What is your objective with all your talks?

I have a single goal: to awaken the sleeping consciousness within us. No one who has attempted this has ever had a different goal; the only objective was to wake up the slumbering consciousness, to awaken the soul within man. Thousands of techniques have been tried to achieve this. Sometimes there would appear to be a contradiction in the methods, but there was never any conflict.

Mahavira and Buddha traveled through the same state, Bihar, at the same time. If you had heard them speak, or the people who heard them… Among you here there might be many people who heard them speak because this is not the first time we have been on the earth. We have been here many times before and will continue to come back many more times in the future. There will be many people who heard Mahavira and Buddha speak and some are present here too – but they may not be aware of it.

Mahavira and Buddha continued traveling in the same state and speaking against each other. People would have been shocked at the strangeness of it all – Buddha and Mahavira contradicting each other! What is the need for them to speak against each other? And they kept on saying harsh things too. Do not think they used gentle words, they were extremely severe.

Buddha often mocked Mahavira. Once Buddha said: "There is one called Niganthnath Putta Mahavira. People say he is all-knowing, but I know for a fact that he goes begging for alms at a house where there is no one inside. Only later, when there is no response to his calls, does he realize that there is no one home. Yet his followers believe that he is all-knowing, omniscient, knows the three worlds." And they kept saying such outrageous things.

Mahavira says that the soul is the only knowledge, soul the only truth, soul the only religion. Soul is the infinite; it is all there is. And what does Buddha say? Buddha says that the soul is ignorance and whoever believes in the soul is bound to go astray; whoever follows the soul will surely slip back. There is no greater ignorance than believing in the soul.

It is very strange: one says the soul is knowledge, the other says the soul is the greatest ignorance. Now we are in a difficult situation. But those who know, know that there is no problem. Buddha has one way, one technique, one method of awakening the consciousness. Mahavira has a different way of doing the same thing. Both have the same goal, only their ways are different.

Mahavira says the soul is knowledge, the soul is everything. And in the same breath he asks: "But when will you know the soul? Only when your ego drops will you be able to realize it. When the ego is no more, then you will know what the soul is." Buddha says: "The soul is ignorance because the soul is the ego. When the soul disappears, only then will you know." But there is no difference between the two.

In India, all the learned people have been declaring that there are an infinite number of lives and for infinite births we have been straying, stagnating, stuck in the same cycle. "How long are you going to keep doing this? Awaken now," they say. On the other hand, Jesus and Mohammed say that there is nothing like infinite births and that there is only one life. They say: "You have only one chance, if you wake up now, you awaken; if not, you have lost the opportunity for ever. Hence, awaken now!"

This is very strange. Here, our teachers say that we have been straying for infinite lives, repeatedly going around in a circle and ask how long we will continue doing so. "Are you not bored? Become bored with all this and awaken now." On the other hand, Jesus and Mohammed say that there is nothing like infinite births, there is only this life. If we miss this, we will miss forever, and there will be no second chance. "If you want to awaken, do so now." Now these statements appear very contradictory, but the people who know realize that it is not so. They say that both are attempts to awaken man from his slumber.

There are contradictions in the words of all the teachers in the world; it will continue to be so. But there will never be any contradiction in their intent. But man's understanding is very limited. People hang on to the words and get confused. They cannot go deeper and determine the truth for what it is.

Another friend has asked:

Osho,
You ask people not to touch your feet. Why?

The reason I ask you not to touch my feet is simply that if you touch anyone's feet, you will miss the opportunity of touching the feet of the divine which is present in all of us. Those feet are everywhere, yet nowhere. Your eyes should be directed toward those feet. Their footsteps can be heard even among the moon and the stars. The flowers and butterflies also echo the sounds of those feet. Among men, and even stones, you can hear the sound of their footsteps. Your hands should be clasped in respect only for those feet which encompass the entire universe. There is no need to bow down to any particular man.

Why? It's not because there is anything wrong in bowing. Bowing is an exceptional experience. Anyone who cannot bow down is not worth two paise, is worthless. But if one has to bow down, let it be to the feet of existence, so that there is never any need to stand up again. Now, if you bow down to touch my feet, a moment later you will have to stand up again – the matter is over. You bent down, and then stood upright again; you wasted your effort. There is no meaning in it, no value.

A man went to Ramakrishna and said to him: "I am going to have a dip in the Ganges. I have heard that if you bathe there, your sins are washed away."

Ramakrishna replied: "Yes, they are washed away. But make sure you do not step out of the river again, because if you do, they will leap back on you. You see those tall trees on the bank of the river? When you go for a dip… The river is holy, so when you go for a dip the sins jump off you and park themselves on the trees. Do you know that this is the reason why those trees are there? They keep sitting there, waiting for you come to out. After all, how long can you stay in the water? After some time you will come out, thinking that the sins have disappeared. But they will jump back on you again.

"Find a river you do not need to step out of. Existence also has its Ganges, and if you immerse yourself in it, that is all there is; there is no way out from there. Even if you want to step out from there, there is nowhere to go – that is all there is."

So I say to you: there are such feet, where if you bow, there is no need to get up again. There is only meaning in paying homage to such feet. If you have to bow down and get up again, it has no meaning; it is worthless.

That is why I say there is no need to bend down. But you will have to bend. This is a very sensitive and delicate matter – don't mistakenly conclude from what I have been saying that you should never bow down. When I ask you not to bow at my feet, some people here may be very happy, thinking that I have said something wonderful. Not because they intend to bow at the feet of existence but because they are uncomfortable bowing before anyone. They will consider my statement correct, absolutely right. Whoever is arrogant will think it perfectly said – agreed, one should not bow.

But I did not say that you shouldn't bow down; I'm only asking you not to bow before *my* feet. Do not mistakenly conclude that I am asking you not to bow at all. I have only told you not to bow needlessly as this kind of bowing is totally useless. What is the meaning of bowing before another man? There is no meaning in it. This body is mere mud, and there is no point in bowing to mud. It is like worshipping mud, and then from this, other wrong practices follow. When the man you were bowing down to disappears, a stone image of him is made and worshipped. Here the practice of bowing down has gone wrong.

No, there is a world full of true knowledge all around, its tentacles spread everywhere. To bend at the feet of existence there is no need to fold your hands, align your feet and bow down your head. Bowing before existence implies an inner suppleness, an inner compliance, a surrender to what is within. Then you have truly bowed down.

And the unique thing is: the person who bows like this never again has to bow because he ceases to regard someone as superior. One who bows at the feet of existence has reached the highest peak, there is nothing higher. Those feet are at such a level, such a peak, that bowing to them does not make you stoop, but lifts you up to even higher levels.

Lao Tzu used to say: "Blessed are they who have bowed, for they will never have to bow." This man is saying a very strange thing, let me repeat it. He says: "Blessed are they who have bowed, for they will never have to bow." Now how is it possible for a man who is already bowing not to bow? Lao Tzu also says: "Blessed are they who have lost, for no one can defeat them." Now how is it possible to again defeat a man who has already been defeated?

The winner is always afraid of losing. Therefore the victorious man is never totally a winner because he has in him the fear of losing. Lao Tzu says that those who have lost are blessed. They have already been defeated, so no one can now defeat them. Blessed are those who are at the rear because there is no place further back for them to go.

But who are these people standing at the rear? Who has defeated them? Those who have bowed before existence have risen, have been lifted up. Those who have surrendered to existence have won; they are victorious. Now there is no possibility of defeat.

Of course I say do not bow at my feet. This notion of my feet, your feet — the very idea of mine and yours – is the obstacle that prevents you from bowing. At the point where the distinction between mine and yours disappears, bowing begins; at that point, you learn how to bow.

So please do not be angry. Some friends have asked me why I have said such a thing; they want to touch my feet. There are very strange habits in our country. If a man says "Do not touch my feet," then it can become a good technique for ensuring that people *do* touch his feet. A very effective trick – if you ask people not to touch your feet, then even more people will want to touch your feet. You ask people to stay away, and they will want to come closer. If you insult them, people will think that this is another great enlightened master. It has been our habit for thousands of years. Cunning and smart people have been exploiting this habit as it appears that a man who asks you not to touch his feet must surely be a great man; his feet should definitely be touched. I do not say this for that reason.

I have said that you must be ready to bow, but not in the wrong place. Bend, bow, as it is the art of being spiritual; fall apart, disappear, vanish, flow away. But where, and for whom? – only at the feet of the infinite, of the universe, of everyone. Bow to that which is all pervasive, is vast, and is present everywhere. But do not bow down to the limited, the shallow, the momentary, which is here today but gone tomorrow.

So keep in mind that I am not against your bowing. Bending is the key, fading away is the key. As long as we are bound rigidly to ourselves and cannot bend, cannot break, we cannot arrive at the place we wish to reach. Disappearing is the key to finding yourself. Losing is the way to winning all. Bowing low is the art of uplifting yourself. But keep in mind where and to what you bow down.

Buddha has narrated an incident from his previous birth:

"During my last birth, when I was not enlightened, not a buddha, and when I did not know and lived in darkness, at that time there was a buddha, a man who had achieved buddhahood. I visited him. I touched his feet, laid my head on his feet. But I had barely stood up when he bent low before me and laid his head on *my* feet.

"I was shocked. I said to him: 'What are you doing? My bowing to you is justified, for I am ignorant. But for you to bow to me – an enlightened one, one who knows, one who has reached – this makes me a sinner. Why did you do such a mad thing?'

"The buddha started laughing, and said to me: 'You

think you are ignorant, but from the moment I came to know, everyone seems to be enlightened. You think you are nobody, but from that time onward, the divine appears to me to be in everyone. You fell at my feet and if I do not in turn fall at your feet, everyone I know will laugh at me. They will say that existence bowed at his feet, but he did not bow to the feet of existence.'

"Then the buddha said: 'You think this way now, but you too will awaken, you will also reach, if not today, then tomorrow. It's only a matter of time, the length of a dream; it is not too long.'

"Now, in my present life, I understand what he told me. Since the time I awakened, to me no one appears to be asleep. Since the time I came to know, I see the divine in everyone."

You ask me why I prevent you from bowing to me. There is only one way for me to allow you: if you touch my feet, I then have to touch your feet. That will create a lot of confusion, a lot of difficulties, it will take a lot of time – and it will all be meaningless. If you greet me with folded hands, it will be very impolite of me not to respond in the same way. It would be very rude of me not to greet you if you have greeted me.

Did you know that in this country, monks do not fold their hands in greeting to anyone? *You* have to greet them with folded hands and only then will they give you their blessings. They will have a photographer waiting nearby who will immediately take a photo. Later a calendar will be published with that photo together with a caption reading that such and such a sage, such and such a monk, is blessing Pandit Nehru. But it's a forgery: out of sheer politeness poor Pandit Nehru greeted the monk with joined hands and the monk didn't even have the courtesy to respond similarly.

If you greet me and I do not greet you, it will be rude, impolite. Exactly in the same way, if you bow at my feet and I do not bow at yours, it is impolite. It is very rude; I have to respond. So now there are only two options – either you agree with me, or you make me work hard! There is no sense in that.

People are not to be worshipped. People should not be worshipped, it should not be permitted. People-worshipping has gone on for long enough and because of it truth cannot be worshipped. Beware of these people. You escape from one person only to be entrapped by another. Be on your guard with such people, avoid them. There is no value in their person; the value is in the truth.

I point to the moon, draw your attention to the moon. But you catch hold of my finger, thinking it is wonderful, and you begin to worship it – the madness starts. I pointed to the moon, but you caught hold of my finger; forgetting the moon, you started praying to my finger.

Mahavira indicates where truth can be found; Jesus cries "Here is the door"; Mohammed says "This is the path – come!" But the Muslims have caught hold of the finger; the Jainas have grabbed it; the Hindus have grasped the finger; the Christians have also seized it – everyone is worshipping the finger. They light lamps, candles and incense sticks, put garlands around the finger and pray to it, declaring it magnificent.

Buddha, Mahavira, Krishna, will all be crying, shedding tears. Whenever they meet in the heavens, they will be sitting together and weeping. They will be hitting their foreheads, wondering what the people they had taught are now doing.

Stop all this; cease doing all this now – there is no need for it. There is no need to worship any man. Forget the signposts; the issue is seeing the moon. Those who want to see the moon will have to go beyond the finger. Your eyes can either be on my finger or looking toward the moon. As soon as you turn your eyes toward the moon, automatically the finger will drop out of sight.

When you go toward the infinite, Mahavira will also drop, Buddha will also drop, Krishna will drop, Ram will drop – all of them will be left behind. They were only signposts on the path, indicating the way.

There are some people here – even intelligent people – who see a milestone showing the way to Mumbai and they clasp that stone close to their chest saying "You are very kind, you have brought me to Mumbai." That poor stone was only a guide, showing the way to Mumbai. It was really telling them to go beyond it in the direction in which it is pointing. But here they are sitting with that stone clasped to their chests. If someone told them to let go of it, they would reply: "Please do not place obstacles in the way of my religion. I am worshipping, I am praying."

No, let go of the man, so that truth can fill the vacuum. Drop everything, so that your eyes can see what can be seen only by eyes that are empty – eyes from which the veil of people, words, scriptures has been lifted, eyes with no curtain of tears in front of them. Only those innocent eyes are able to see the ultimate truth.

Finding this truth, touching the shadow of this truth, is known as finding peace. Whoever finds this truth becomes totally calm, at last finds tranquility. Find truth and like a shadow, peace will follow. The shadow of truth is peace.

So do not try to find peace directly. If you invite me to your home, my shadow will also come, even without an invitation; there is no need to invite it separately. But if you invite only my shadow, then you know what to expect: I will not come and my shadow cannot come.

People who invite only peace will never find peace. Peace is the shadow of truth. When truth comes, peace follows it like a shadow.

During these four days, I have spoken a little about finding this truth so that you may also find peace. I am very grateful to you for listening to me with so much love and patience. Finally, I offer my greetings to the godliness that dwells in all of us. Please accept my greetings.

About Osho

Osho's unique contribution to the understanding of who we are defies categorization. Mystic and scientist, a rebellious spirit whose sole interest is to alert humanity to the urgent need to discover a new way of living. To continue as before is to invite threats to our very survival on this unique and beautiful planet.

His essential point is that only by changing ourselves, one individual at a time, can the outcome of all our "selves" – our societies, our cultures, our beliefs, our world – also change. The doorway to that change is meditation.

Osho the scientist has experimented and scrutinized all the approaches of the past and examined their effects on the modern human being and responded to their short-comings by creating a new starting point for the hyperactive 21st Century mind: OSHO Active Meditations.

Once the agitation of a modern lifetime has started to settle, "activity" can melt into "passivity," a key starting point of real meditation. To support this next step, Osho has transformed the ancient "art of listening" into a subtle contemporary methodology: the OSHO Talks. Here words become music, the listener discovers who is listening, and the awareness moves from what is being heard to the individual doing the listening. Magically, as silence arises, what needs to be heard is understood directly, free from the distraction of a mind that can only interrupt and interfere with this delicate process.

These thousands of talks cover everything from the

individual quest for meaning to the most urgent social and political issues facing society today. Osho's books are not written but are transcribed from audio and video recordings of these extemporaneous talks to international audiences. As he puts it, "So remember: whatever I am saying is not just for you…I am talking also for the future generations."

Osho has been described by *The Sunday Times* in London as one of the "1000 Makers of the 20th Century" and by American author Tom Robbins as "the most dangerous man since Jesus Christ." *Sunday Mid-Day* (India) has selected Osho as one of ten people – along with Gandhi, Nehru and Buddha – who have changed the destiny of India.

About his own work Osho has said that he is helping to create the conditions for the birth of a new kind of human being. He often characterizes this new human being as "Zorba the Buddha" – capable both of enjoying the earthy pleasures of a Zorba the Greek and the silent serenity of a Gautama the Buddha.

Running like a thread through all aspects of Osho's talks and meditations is a vision that encompasses both the timeless wisdom of all ages past and the highest potential of today's (and tomorrow's) science and technology.

Osho is known for his revolutionary contribution to the science of inner transformation, with an approach to meditation that acknowledges the accelerated pace of contemporary life. His unique OSHO Active Meditations[™] are designed to first release the accumulated stresses of body and mind, so that it is then easier to take an experience of stillness and thought-free relaxation into daily life.

Two autobiographical works by the author are available:
Autobiography of a Spiritually Incorrect Mystic,
St Martins Press, New York (book and eBook)
Glimpses of a Golden Childhood,
OSHO Media International, Pune, India
(book and eBook)

OSHO International Meditation Resort

Each year the Meditation Resort welcomes thousands of people from more than 100 countries. The unique campus provides an opportunity for a direct personal experience of a new way of living – with more awareness, relaxation, celebration and creativity. A great variety of around-the-clock and around-the-year program options are available. Doing nothing and just relaxing is one of them!

All of the programs are based on Osho's vision of "Zorba the Buddha" – a qualitatively new kind of human being who is able *both* to participate creatively in every-day life *and* to relax into silence and meditation.

Location
Located 100 miles southeast of Mumbai in the thriving modern city of Pune, India, the OSHO International Meditation Resort is a holiday destination with a difference. The Meditation Resort is spread over 28 acres of spectacular gardens in a beautiful tree-lined residential area.

OSHO Meditations
A full daily schedule of meditations for every type of person includes both traditional and revolutionary methods, and particularly the OSHO Active Meditations™. The daily meditation program takes place in what must be the world's largest meditation hall, the OSHO Auditorium.

OSHO Multiversity

Individual sessions, courses and workshops cover everything from creative arts to holistic health, personal transformation, relationship and life transition, transforming meditation into a lifestyle for life and work, esoteric sciences, and the "Zen" approach to sports and recreation. The secret of the OSHO Multiversity's success lies in the fact that all its programs are combined with meditation, supporting the understanding that as human beings we are far more than the sum of our parts.

OSHO Basho Spa

The luxurious Basho Spa provides for leisurely open-air swimming surrounded by trees and tropical green. The uniquely styled, spacious Jacuzzi, the saunas, gym, tennis courts...all these are enhanced by their stunningly beautiful setting.

Cuisine

A variety of different eating areas serve delicious Western, Asian and Indian vegetarian food – most of it organically grown especially for the Meditation Resort. Breads and cakes are baked in the resort's own bakery.

Night life

There are many evening events to choose from – dancing being at the top of the list! Other activities include full-moon meditations beneath the stars, variety shows, music performances and meditations for daily life.

Facilities

You can buy all of your basic necessities and toiletries in the Galleria. The Multimedia Gallery sells a large range of OSHO media products. There is also a bank, a travel agency and a Cyber Café on-campus. For those who enjoy shopping, Pune provides all the options, ranging from traditional and ethnic Indian products to all of the global brand-name stores.

Accommodation
You can choose to stay in the elegant rooms of the OSHO Guesthouse, or for longer stays on campus you can select one of the OSHO Living-In programs. Additionally there is a plentiful variety of nearby hotels and serviced apartments.

www.osho.com/meditationresort
www.osho.com/guesthouse
www.osho.com/livingin

For More Information

www.**OSHO**.com

a comprehensive multi-language website including a magazine, OSHO Books, OSHO Talks in audio and video formats, the OSHO Library text archive in English and Hindi and extensive information about OSHO Meditations. You will also find the program schedule of the OSHO Multiversity and information about the OSHO International Meditation Resort.

http://OSHO.com/AllAboutOSHO
http://OSHO.com/Resort
http://OSHO.com/Shop
http://www.youtube.com/OSHO
http://www.Twitter.com/OSHO
http://www.facebook.com/pages/OSHO.International

To contact OSHO International Foundation:
www.osho.com/oshointernational,
oshointernational@oshointernational.com